Champion Bissell

**The panic, as seen from Parnassus : and other poems**

Champion Bissell

**The panic, as seen from Parnassus : and other poems**

ISBN/EAN: 9783743328716

Manufactured in Europe, USA, Canada, Australia, Japa

Cover: Foto ©ninafisch / pixelio.de

Manufactured and distributed by brebook publishing software (www.brebook.com)

Champion Bissell

**The panic, as seen from Parnassus : and other poems**

# THE PANIC,

## AS SEEN FROM PARNASSUS;

### AND

# OTHER POEMS,

BY

## CHAMPION BISSELL.

———

——Stulta est clementia, quum tot ubique
Vatibus occurras, periturae parcere chartae.
*Juvenal.*

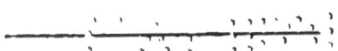

NEW YORK:
T. J. CROWEN, No. 699 BROADWAY.
MDCCCLX.

# CONTENTS.

|  | PAGE |
|---|---|
| THE PANIC, | 1 |
| "LOOK OUT UPON THE SUNLIT WAVES," | 34 |
| THE PAPER-MILL, | 35 |
| EPIGRAMS FROM MARTIAL, | 39 |
| ORION, | 42 |
| H. C. H., | 45 |
| SIR WALTER, | 46 |
| ANTI-ARCADIAN, | 48 |
| MARGARITA SPOLIATRIX, | 52 |
| HARTFORD, | 57 |
| NEW ENGLAND HOUSES, | 58 |
| CHILDHOOD, | 61 |
| COLLEGE, | 66 |
| EPIGRAMS FROM MARTIAL, | 75 |
| THE POET'S PRAYER, | 78 |
| THE MILL-WHEEL, | 80 |
| HINTS FROM THE SIXTH SATIRE, | 82 |
| ADVICE, | 106 |
| EPIGRAMS FROM MARTIAL, | 107 |
| AROOSTOOK, | 110 |
| AT MANILLA, | 111 |
| OVID—PARIS AD HELENAM, | 113 |
| HELENA AD PARIDEM, | 133 |

## CONTENTS.

|  | PAGE |
|---|---|
| LOVE'S FINDING, | 147 |
| TEDIUM VITÆ, | 159 |
| TO A DAY IN MARCH, | 164 |
| LUCY, | 166 |
| THE STREAM AT THE NORTH, | 169 |
| GALLIA CAPTA, | 174 |
| EPIGRAMS FROM MARTIAL, | 176 |
| SOPHIA, | 177 |
| A FINANCIAL EXPERIENCE, | 184 |
| CROSS PURPOSES, | 190 |
| ROSALIA, | 191 |
| HELEN, | 201 |
| SONNET, | 204 |
| "SWIFT RUSHING RIVER OF LIFE," | 205 |
| "WHAT LESSON GRAVES THOSE HOARY ROCKS?" | 206 |
| FRAGMENTS FROM HORACE: | |
|     AD LICINIUM, | 207 |
|     AD FUSCUM, | 209 |
| HOMER, | 211 |
| MILTON, | 212 |
| SHAKSPEARE, | 213 |
| CYRILLA, | 216 |

# POEMS.

# THE PANIC,

## As Seen from Parnassus.

A RHYMED LETTER TO A COUNTRY COUSIN.

Dear Cousin Walter, in your pleasant world
Beside the Susquehanna's azure flow,
Where mountain upon mountain rudely hurled
Casts kindly shadows on the plains below,
What care to you, the commerce-fevered mart,
The schemes of trade devised by human art,
The ebbs and floods of wealth, the city's haste,
The streams of gold that poison all who taste,
The creditor's demand, the law's delay,
The rushing crowds, the quick and eager day,
The fitful hopes, and chances of the game,
Where merchants gamble for success or shame—
What care to you are these?  Your lot is cast
Where these, like idle rumors, hurry past;

Content to share the gifts that Nature yields,
The ruler sole of wide and fruitful fields.

Happy your life. For all not thus await
The peaceful pleasures of the rural state.
Necessity hath arms no tyrant knows:
And where she urges, who shall hope repose?
She drives amid the fearful ranks of men,
And scatters them with pitiless force apart;
Nor shall they dream of quietness again,
While she pursues them with relentless heart.
Ah! who shall say in Youth's delighted years,
When all the future robed in white appears:
Here will I fix my constant, sure abode,
Nor venture on the steep, laborious road
Where men the Pilgrimage to Fortune make,
And bleed and pant for her deceitful sake!
Too empty boast—the destined hour shall come,
Her haughty summons call thee swift away—
As when to action beats the soldier-drum,
Let none dare linger—death awaits delay!

But let me not, too mournful, pen the theme
Which you shall ponder by your peaceful stream;

For in the city's fierce and anxious strife,
Some rays of pleasure still illume our life:
Though custom-trammeled, and the slaves of gain,
Our manners, morals, smirched with foreign stain;
Though cursed with rulers vile beyond belief—
The sport of gambler, mountebank, and thief—
Justice a fugitive and Law a jest—
He least regarded who is called the best;
Though Trade precarious mock the wisest care,
And dissipate our bankrupt toil in air;
Though noxious vapors fill our summer sky,
And Europe's plagues instruct us how to die—
Still we survive—some comfort still extract
From boding fancy and from direful fact.

Erewhile the city mad with plenty grew,
When the last full decade was fresh and new;
When, first awakened from his long repose,
The giant Commerce shook himself and rose.
And first he called to all the fruitful land
To pour its harvests on th' Atlantic strand.
For this he stretched the iron rail afar,
And launched for this the swift capacious car;

Taught distant Iowa to send her grain
(That else unbought had wasted on the plain)
To feed the famine of a foreign host,
And make our fruits a blessing and a boast.
Nor was the stirring summons disobeyed :
Quick to the sea the bounteous burden sped,
And ocean groaned beneath the countless sail
That bore abundance with the western gale.

Why should I speak of ships whose sudden birth
Surpassed the wonders of the April earth?
Their growth beginning with a summer's sun—
Launched on the waters ere his course was run!
Complete in beauty rose the shapely hull,
Tapering the bow, the waist more round and full ;
While to the rear, the lines, retreating in,
Recalled the magic of the dolphin's fin.
The masts, far reaching to the upper blue,
Yet straight as lance, and tough as Saxon yew,
Bore spreading acres of adventurous sail,
To woo the zephyr or withstand the gale.
These miracles romantic names adorn—
Pride of the Seas ; The Wave ; The Shining Morn ;

The Ocean-Tamer; Monarch of the Spray;
Great Neptune's Chariot; Purple Dawn of Day!
Once the calm Greek in marble carved the line,
And wrought perfection in an Art Divine;
Once rapt Italians drew the Master's face,
And vested painting with unearthly grace;
But in the rush of this our wondrous time,
Our ardor made Utility sublime,
And fixed the aspirations of the soul
In those creations, all unknown before,
Which, wafted whereso'er the oceans roll,
Conveyed our genius to the farthest shore.
The generous frenzy who shall dare lament—
Haply with folly and with rashness blent?
No; if o'er sordid traffic Fancy fling
Her kindly graces with expansive wing;
If she adorn the arts that thus subserve
The needs of men, she ever shall deserve
Our grateful homage, and the praise shall find
Of all who truly, justly, love mankind.

While thus abroad the Land her harvest flung,
The scales of Commerce even-balanced hung;

And justly with profusion then we drew
The wealth of Europe, and her luxuries too.
Proud is the sceptre of a virgin state
That feeds the nations at her bounteous gate,
Deigns to accept the rich exchange they bring,
As queens receive a subject's offering;
Smiles on the busy arts her plenty cheers,
And reads bright omens in the coming years.

Exhaustless seemed the store at our command,
Though scattered freely with a tireless hand.
The wondrous staple of the Southern clime,
Material ruler of our race and time,
Whose ebb and flow of value through the world
Are more significant and vast to men,
Than if Napoleon's throne be downward hurled,
Or Hapsburgh tumble, ne'er to rise again;
The golden berry of the prairied West,
Favorite of earth and fruit of double years,
The topaz-gem that shines on Ceres' breast,
When flushed with early autumn she appears:
These, with a lesser host, but equal sum—
From piny forests, aromatic gum;

The offspring white of Carolina's fen;
The dark-hued weed, whose cloud-compelling power
Enslaves, and cheers, and soothes, and conquers men,
And charms the reveries of the listless hour:
These were our riches; these the busy tide
Of commerce wafted outward far and wide;
And that our hands might ever kindly pour,
Suppliant, the Nations thronged about our door.

Then woke the people to a higher need,
And wants began to stir, till then unknown.
Why lose the birthright—why the destined meed
Forego, nor claim the rights that were our own?
To us belong the spoils of other lands,
And what is fairest, wrought by foreign hands—
The silk, the purple, linen, fruit, and oil;
The flowing blood of red Burgundy's soil;
Robes from the Orient, spices from Kathay;
The webs that cheat the burning Indian day;
The sturdy fabric of the moorland mill,
The sum of Flemish craft and Saxon skill:
Nay, all that centuries of weary toil
Have slowly ripened on a foreign soil,

Here to our dawning land shall instant throng,
And find the lords to whom they all belong.
Here burns the Star of Empire: here confessed
Is found the King shall rule o'er all the rest.

Such was the general sense; the private soul
Felt the same passion that inspired the whole;
A thirst for wealth, that quickly, madly grew,
But not for industry and temperance too..
As truants, when some golden fruit they see,
Forget the owner's toil that raised the tree,
Crave the fair treasure, leap the garden-wall,
And brave the trap, the ditch, the watch-dog's call;
So we, in haste to grasp the glittering prize
That danced on high before our eager eyes,
Leaped every bound; although, for virtue's sake,
We spared—whate'er we had no power to take.

Through every house the quick contagion spread:
In air we breathed it—ate it with our bread.
Old things were past; the new before us lay,
Warm o'er us beamed the sun of Fortune's day.
Loosed from their bounds, outburst our fierce desires,
And flamed in countless and in lawless fires;

And scorning toil, but loving what it brought,
From others' sweat, our own repose we sought.


Why speak of schemes, begot with every sun,
Whose paths were many, but their purpose one?
The BANK, whose shares, on bright crisp paper wrote,
Were based upon the PROMISSORY NOTE—
Sublimest fiction of the age of brass,
Where borrowers organized to lend each other,
And safely trusted that the Public Ass
Would prove to them a kindly nursing mother!
Where men, scarce competent to write their name,
Whose only talent was a lack of shame,
Filled the financial presidential chair,
And, each a bankrupt, played the millionaire;
Where thieves well drilled and banded into hordes,
Styled by the public prints, DIRECTION BOARDS,
Met twice a week or oftener, and divided
The funds their duped depositors provided;
The GRAND STOCK COMPANY, for each design,
Where schemers, swindlers, rascals, could combine:

The growth of tea upon the coast of Maine,
In warm Vermont the tropic sorghum-cane;
The manufacture, by a process rare,
Of ice from common atmospheric air—
The plan is still extant—'tis not pretense—
The only trouble is, it won't condense;
The Company for warming every house,
For roasting private joints or parish gruel,
Humble corned-beef, aristocratic grouse,
Without the aid of gas, or stove, or fuel;
The Building Company, a wondrous plan,
For fifty cents a week the poorest man
Might, by its certain, magical expansion,
Become the owner of a park and mansion;
But ere this time, too short for me to say,
The treasurer was sure to run away!
The Grand Association for returning
Smoke into coal—Experimental Burning
Reduced the capital so very low,
At last there wasn't even smoke to show:
The Great Insurance Scheme—a novel feature—
Commends itself to every living creature,

Insures your house, your income, or your life,
Your cashier's books, the honor of your wife,
Insures your debts—nay, for a round commission
Would undertake to get your sins remission.

But chief of all, the mammoth RAILROAD DODGE
Absorbed the mind of Dives and of Hodge:
Nor was the scheme unmixed with sober sense—
A healthy core, o'ergrown with rank pretense.
Shall I revive the records of the day
That frittered credit, fortune, hopes, away?
Nay, more—devoured the widow's slender purse,
And made the orphan outcast—or a worse?
Fain would I hope the slow, reluctant muse
Should sing some feeble strains of lasting use;
Some strains that, floating past the present hour,
Shall have in future days a warning power.
But who shall say? The lessons of the time
Though fixed in annals—crystallized in rhyme—
Like stars whose distant, faint, and glimmering light
Warms not the sense, although it reach the sight;
But coldly, feebly touch an after-age,
Whose blood is warmer than the printed page.

Nay, if the felon's shame be branded in,
His children's children none the less shall sin!
What age is wiser for the age that's past?
The newest folly still repeats the last:
And though no wave of air that mortals draw
Has not borne freight of Gospel and of law
Still runs the world its sad and motley round,
And sins and follies none the less abound!


Thus we explain the madness that possessed
One half the nation, and amazed the rest—
That threw the ponderous chain of iron road
O'er lonely plains where man had scarcely trod!
As if the long-drawn lines of rusted bar,
The jangling rattle of the empty car,
Had magic potence to produce the birth
Of full-grown cities from the lonely earth;
As if the secret of the wealth of states,
Long hid from mortal eyes by envious fates,
Were now revealed, as if by sudden shock,
To wondering eyes, in form of Railroad Stock!

As toward the rich, inviting spoils of Rome,
The fierce Barbarian, weary of his home—
Of countless marchings on the frozen plain;
Of chill encampment by the Baltic main;
Of Scythian rigors, boundless glooms of pine,
And fruitless fishing in the icy Rhine—
Looked out, and longed, and clanged his brazen shield,
And called his comrades to th' Italian field:
So, if the ancient story do not shame
The base ignoble raid I blush to name,
From every village, every petty town,
A swarm of thieves and jobbers hastened down
To where the toil of twice a hundred years
In evidence of golden fruit appears.
With care and sweat, six broods of patient men
Had made a garden on the Eastern main.
Six generations slowly fading hence,
Had left bequest of peaceful competence.
In wise contentment we possessed the store
Thus heritaged, nor rashly wished it more;
Content to wait on Nature's certain laws,
That fasten means to end—effect to cause;

Sure, if we labored, that her warm increase
Would blossom forth in kindly wealth and peace.

What lying arts, what treachery and stealth,
Were then employed to cheat us of our wealth!
Uncounted tales of distant states and lands,
Whose riches vied with Sacramento's sands;
Of cities waiting for the iron track
To pour their plenty in, and take our traffic back.
Such cities! Let the time-worn Eastern coast,
New York and Boston, and such other, boast;
Reared on a barren and a hostile soil,
And only rich by prodigies of toil:
But there, within deep-margined plenty set,
Are Keokuk, Racine, and Joliet:
Kenosha, Madison, and Battle Creek—
I think the six were built within a week!—
Dubuque and Davenport, and classic Cairo—
The last was lately swallowed by the high ro-
Mantic waters of that sparkling stream,
Whose silver waves would grace a poet's dream—
I mean the Mississippi! if you strain it
For several days, *some* stomachs can retain it!—

And last, a place where debtors let the law go,
Nor fear their Eastern creditors—Chicago.

"These proud creations of our Western skill,
With rich rewards your pockets long to fill,
On these conditions: buy our railroad stock;
Supply each lake-port with a marble dock;
Purchase our farms and fences, right of way;
The cord-wood of the State with ready pay,
To keep the engines going; when, quite sick
Of credit, Chop declines to sell on tick,
Then take our bonds—a very easy load—
Not more than twice the value of the road!
And then—we own it seems a trifle funny—
We want to borrow certain sums of money
Upon the income that the roads will bring,
When once we fix and finish up the thing.
For though—and here we pledge our solemn word—
We're richer than the world has ever heard.
Still, just at present, owing to the smash
In Western lands, we *are* quite short of cash.
But as the roads are built, the lands will rise,
And then 'tis plain to your sagacious eyes,

Your funds will safe return whence they were sent,
With rich increase of twenty-four per cent.
Nor think that we nor fear nor reverence law—
We drink in virtue with the breath we draw!
When Western debtors fly, and can't be found,
Or Western city fails to pay its bond,
Or Western Railroad shirks its due coupon—
Where *is* the road that ever tried it on?—
Then—not till then—what we require, deny us;
For our expansive country's sake, oh! try us!"

Says Butler—not exact do I repeat—
To cheated be, is merrier than to cheat.
Such our philosophy—with pleaséd grin,
We sucked the bait of Western cheatery in.
From our strong boxes took the guardian lock,
And changed the contents into railroad stock.
It took less room—was easier to hold—
Was "more convertible," they said, "than gold!"
They found it so; but this is to be said of it:
The faculty quite ceased when they got rid of it;
And he who now "converts" a Western bond,
Possesses powers evangelists' beyond!

Alas! how few escaped the fatal snare—
The Lawyer, Parson, Doctor, all were there;
The Ploughman sold his plough and bought a share!
The Merchant sold his stock of goods for stock,
Mynheer his farm; the Yankee sold his clock!
The Schoolma'am from the Bank her savings drew;
The shrewd and sly Cashier invested too.
I merely state the fact, and mean it kindly,
The whole male population rushed in blindly;
The women followed—those who had the means,
And bonds and stocks went off in solid reams!

This was the climax—as the years went by,
We slowly woke to see how vast the lie;
Yet so prodigious, we could scarce believe
That human genius could so far deceive;
And when the Money column gravely stated,
That " Grabtown, Iowa, repudiated,"
The kindly holders sent a letter out,
And mildly " hoped the thing would come about."
Such lenience might have fused a rock—despite it,
All Grabtown published that " they meant to fight
    it;

They had the best of counsel—they would see
If Eastern capital could chain the free!"
Nor they alone, for over all the land
Repudiation raised its dirty hand!
It sickens one of man and human nature,
To note the movements of this filthy creature;
How, though abhorrent to the single breast,
It finds among a crowd a ready nest;
And those who brag of honor, with each other
Loudly conspire a righteous claim to smother!

But when we fully knew the vile deceit,
And men grew bold to call a cheat, a cheat,
Then o'er the land's whole breadth arose the sense
Of present poverty and impotence.
How much we owed abroad, that larger grew
With every cargo to our ports that flew!
Our ships were idle; prospering sun and rain
Had filled all Europe with abundant grain.
Back to the towns, the wasted farms returned
Hosts of gaunt laborers—Man by Nature spurned!
Sublimest satire on our social state,
When fields their natural lord repudiate,

With fatal justice full revenges take,
And by him paupered, him a pauper make!

Nor this alone, for every honest trade
Felt the vast burden that our debts had made,
And—'tis the olden tale, and sad as brief—
First flew to Shylock to obtain relief.
Scarce will you credit the usurious tale—
Should fancy falter, figures never fail—
From off the face of every fair exchange,
From ten to twenty let the discount range;
Then double this, wherever pressing need
Or scanty time compelled the instant deed;
Yet shall you safely keep within the rate
That bore on labor with such crushing weight!

Nor long could this exhausting aid endure—
To such relief the end is always sure;
Through the wide country, through the pent-up
    town,
Headlong the smaller traders toppled down:
Each shrinking wretch who thus received his fate,
Involved another, haply twice as great;

Nor by his debts alone—a general fear
Each one of others, shook the business sphere,
Disturbed its elements, and scattered thence
The kindly grounds of hope and confidence;
Filled with a false suspicion every breast,
And robbed the day of peace, the night of rest.


So passed the early summer of the year,
When August came, and brought the PANIC near.
In fear of some unseen impending woe,
A vague alarm of some relentless foe,
Men came and went, till on one gloomy day
The cloud that hid the Evil, broke away.
A Mammoth Company, whose business spanned
From far Ohio to th' Atlantic strand,
Within whose yawning coffers had been poured
Unnumbered mites by helpless widows stored—
The clerk's small savings and the merchant's gains,
The rich man's titles to his vast domains—
At once, and utterly—forever—sank;
Its notes six millions—nothing in the Bank!

I well remember how, with features paled,
The feverish multitudes went home that day,
Their thought—Since that Great Company has failed,
All hopes are vain, let ruin have its way:
Let ruin rule, this be my only care,
To shun the evils that my friends must share;
Be still, my warm emotions; let me steel
My heart, that else the kindly throb might feel:
A struggling swimmer, shall I weakly think
To share my spar with him who else might sink?
Or, scarcely floating in my frail canoe—
A risk to one, but certain death to two—
Extend the oar to any luckless wight
Who faintly battles with the storm and night?

Nor did the grim suspicion fail to rise:
Since Honor oft in time of trial dies,
Will those whom I have known and counted true—
In fair and prosperous days, alas! how few!—
Stand by their virtue when temptations call,
Be firmly honest, though the heavens fall?
If such I doubt, they doubt the same of me;
Is doubt, then, shadow of Reality?

As when, by common impulse, famine-led,
A flock of pigeons, flying o'er your head,
Hastes to the nearest wheat-field, there to find
Their neighbor flocks in rivalry combined;
Then if they seek another, lo! the air
Is black with hungry pigeons hurrying there;
And soaring upward to the utmost height,
Still see no vacant spot to tempt their flight—
So, when to sore financial famine brought,
The nearest Bank some swarm of merchants sought,
They found the parlor, hall, already crammed,
The tired Cashier behind his table jammed,
The ancient President in close blockade,
And warmest siege around the lobbies laid;
Before, a crowd; behind, a long procession;
And scarcely room to force a retrogression.
Then, if they sought a Bank in distant street,
With panting breath and sorely blistered feet,
Still were they sure a frantic crowd to meet;
Till wearied with the hot and useless chase,
Each struggler sought his own accustomed place—
And grim Despair was there, and looked him in
    the face!

But could each one have said his eager say,
Of what avail were Banks to such as they?
The Earth no causeless Panic e'er did breed,
And debts are plants that always spring from seed!
To aid the fair exchange of man with man
By bridging Time—the true financial plan:
But not to bolster up a sinking cause;
Not to assist in spurning prudent laws;
Not to find capital for reckless men,
Their only stock in hand, th' indorsing pen,
Who waste each night the winnings of the day,
And leave their creditors their debts to pay;
Nor yet to prop the dubious enterprise—
Though haply chance success may stamp it wise—
Of sanguine, ardent spirits, rash and bold,
Who venture freely, nobly, others' gold;
If lucky, pay; if broke, with heat declaim
Against the hapless turn of Fortune's stream,
Just at the very moment when Success
Was hastening on, their enterprise to bless!

Nay, more—to blame the Banks for our distress
Nor helps our cause, nor makes our folly less:

For does the banker's loan create a claim
That he shall always thence renew the same?
Because he once extends a kind advance,
Must he for ever feed extravagance?
And if it come to this, 'tis plainly shown
The Banks had risked their safety for our own.
For months, the Trader to the Banker flew:
For months, the loan in rapid increase grew;
Nor did the merchant slacken his demand:
The treasures borrowed from the Banker's hand,
But fed his appetite for more, and still
His wants appeared more vast—more hard to fill.

What wonder, then, that self-defense compelled
The golden stream should be an hour withheld?
I grant some error—who is always wise?
The skilled physician not at once denies
To him who writhes in fierce delirium's pain,
The poisonous draught that nursed it in his brain;
But slowly, surely, safely, leads him back,
Retracing up the scorched and lurid track.
Here was the path of wisdom; well, had they,
The Banks, but read the lesson of the day;

Then milder were the punishment of all,
And Fortune's blessings easier to recall.


Oh! who can e'er forget the long-drawn ranks
That 'sieged the discount counters of the Banks?
In single file the gloomy squadron stood,
Like famine-wasted men scarce hoping food!
They stretched across the room, they doubled in;
They turned and came, and went and came again;
They ran beyond the doors; the noonday heat
Beheld them standing in the glaring street;
And still the sad procession longer grew,
Till where it ended, no one cared or knew.


Hope more forlorn has never stormed a wall,
Where one dread ruin lies in store for all!
The books were scarcely opened: "Nothing done,"
Why need be said to all, when said to one?
But still each hopeless wretch a duty thought,
That his last offering should at least be brought;
Then if he failed, of him should not be said,
"Without a struggle has he joined the dead!"

Then sank the merchant princes—every day
Some old and giant house forebore to pay.
The lesser stars that dropped from out the sky,
No one remarked them—they of course must die;
But every eye was fixed upon the fall
Of luminaries that had dazed us all:
Still one by one they tumbled, till the bare
Expanse of space but showed us where they were!

As in some direful siege, the gossip's talk,
The casual meeting, and the stealthy walk,
All insufficient prove to tell the world
How many victims into death are hurled;
Then day by day the sad funereal list
Reveals the killed, the wounded, and the missed:
So, 'mid the slaughter of the Panic, we
Received the black list of necrology.
Weekly 'twas published, constant there we read
The once-familiar titles of the dead;
There every Thursday, going home to dine,
We spelled the captions bristling down the line;
And—were the prophets to the earth recalled?—
The dread intelligence was oft forestalled:

Oft was the cheek of shrinking merchant paled
To read that he was numbered with the failed,
When, with his ensign flying at the peak,
He yet had steam to ride the waves a week!

But news is news, no matter what the theme,
And men will drink, though turbid be the stream:
This wretched catalogue a luxury grew
And those who sought and read it not, were few.
And as, upon the Fourth of each July,
The schoolboy throws his books and satchel by,
Cheers his great grandsires whom he never saw,
And fires the cracker, and rebounds the taw;
So we observed—but in a dismal way—
The coming in of "Independent's" day!

But as the deadly catalogue increased,
And confidence and credit waned and ceased;
As stocks went down and down, and out of sight,
Engulfed in ruin and in hopeless night;
As men who lately ruled the world's exchange,
And taught the markets of the continent
The proper measure of their daily range,
Faint-hearted grew, and feared each day's event;

The public wavered in the faith it kept
In Wall-street vaults in which their treasures slept;
And as upon some lowering day in spring,
From out the clouds, the northern tempests fling
Sudden destruction o'er the shivering plain,
And rend the blossom, crush the tender grain;
So sudden, sharp, and deadly was the blast
Of public anger that arose at last
Against the Banks; and scarce a private soul
But nursed some secret grudge against the whole.
Here one had humbly, in some hour of need—
Compelled against his pride for aid to plead—
Pleaded, and vainly; and his wounded breast
Now hailed revenge, and taught it to the rest.
Here one had suffered a dishonored name;
Long had he struggled to avert the shame—
Another month, a week, perhaps a day,
Would bring him aid: will not the Bank delay?
The hope, how idle! Fortune now the case
Had changed; and now he wore another face:
His time had come to claim, and loudly too;
And as he once had sued, now they should sue.

Here one had felt a real or fancied slight;
Here one had vainly tried the adventurous kite;
Here one who used the Bank, as thieves the "fence,"
Convenient cloak to screen his own pretense—
At last detected in his dirty snares,
And—fit chastisement—hustled down the stairs,
*He* had his grievance too, harangued the crowd,
His virtue vehement, his language loud;
And still he talked, and still they cheered, and higher
Flashed up the folly-fed and angry fire.

But why recount the sources of the flame
That burned within the breasts of all who came
To storm the treasures which themselves had stored,
And risk the safety of the common hoard?
Whatever wisdom lodges with a mob
Who haply meet, to burn, to sack, to rob,
Be sure was there, and there you too might find
Of what a city rabble is combined;
Nor wholly rabble, for the fierce event
Had brought the city out by one consent;
The swart mechanic, and the well-dressed clerk,
The unknown laborer, and the man of mark;

The rich retired merchant, anxious he
As aught the poorest wretch, his gold to see;
The lawyer, broker, active man of trade.
But chief the vast and seething crowd was made
Of that great restless mass of human souls—
*Vulgus ignobile*—a swarm of moles—
Each known by some one—sister, wife, or mother;
But met in crowds—and no man knows another!


The first day's work was tasteful, neat, and light—
Three banks they smashed—then parted for the
  night.
This put them well in training—was the wine
That boxers take, an hour before they dine.
But when arose the red October's sun
Of the next morning, work was fresh begun.
Each panting, eager warrior broke his fast,
As if that day's first meal might prove the last,
And donned his warlike beaver, and went down
To where the sacred spires o'er Wall street frown,
Prepared with check and note for conflict dire—
Thus flamed within each breast a common fire!

Within, uneasy tellers counted o'er
The wasted remnants of their golden store,
And tried—but vainly tried—to make them more.
The food of war is ammunition, here,
As where Bellona shakes her gory spear.
But though they wadding had, enough for all,
Their stock of metal was but wondrous small;
Their specious promises were far from being
The specie that the crowd was bent on seeing;
And though their charges often had been large,
How did they falter when they met the charge!

Fast pressed the multitude, the Teller's hands
Pay out and pay, but still the crowd demands:
I mean the Paying Teller, for the other
Experienced not the least degree of bother;
Calm at his bench he sat—the gay deceiver,
Who naught received, yet styled himself Receiver,
And read the morning's news—and chaffed the rabble,
And laughed at all their senseless, noisy babble,
Alone, of all unmoved. The pale Cashier
Moved up and down the Bank in ceaseless fear;

The President, within his private room,
Refused access, and gave himself to gloom;
And one raised blood, and one was carried home!
But still the surging crowd went in and out,
While from the streets arose an endless shout.

Unequal contest—where the mob combine
To break the image or destroy the shrine!
The title of the god be what it may,
The public will is sure to have its way.
So was it now: each slowly waning hour,
Bank after Bank succumbed to lawless power,
Confessed itself a bankrupt, closed the gate;
And quite relieved of all its heavy weight
Of care and coin, consigned itself to Fate.
The crowd subsided then; the stroke of four
Found Wall street empty as the lone sea-shore,
And still; as after storm subsides the watery roar.

As often tempests clear the summer air
Of plagues and death, that else had sheltered there,
So this fierce outbreak of the mob dispersed
The brooding evils that the time had nursed.
For this, no praise—if madness foster good,
Still be the true connection understood;

For reason, patient, following down the path
Where public folly closed in public wrath,
The folly senseless—but the anger more—
Deduced the lessons that the history bore;
The lessons old as man's exchanging art,
Learned through all time by every prudent heart,
Garnered in Writ by Solomon the wise,
Traced through the ages as they upward rise,
Nursed by the liberal mind, they blossom thence
In Franklin's maxims—Bacon's lucid sense.

Two years have gone; the PANIC long has passed,
And we forget the ills that cease to blast;
A prospering sun returns, and we at length
Feel the kind symptoms of reviving strength;
But if our sinews, not as yet restored
To that full power whose loss we late deplored,
Too early tempt the lavish, boundless strain,
Then were our former suffering all in vain;
And sharper sorrows shall the truth recall,
That pride o'erweening ever hastes to fall;
That states are strongest when but slowly made,
And Justice strikes when Nature's disobeyed.

Look out upon the sunlit waves, and say
That they will smile to-morrow, as to-day.
Oh! no, you cannot. Clouds will haply rise,
Or rains descend from out the changeful skies;
Or, driving shoreward from th' Atlantic deep,
Chill, sullen mists shall o'er the waters creep.

Perhaps to-day, the bloom of many a flower
Is at its gorgeous full—its final hour;
Perhaps to-day, the sweetest, fullest song,
That e'er charmed echo loved to bear along,
Is for the last time sung: the eager dawn
Wakes but to find the song and minstrel gone.

## THE PAPER-MILL.

This is the paper-mill—you heard
    The humming as we turned the ridge,
Where, lightly lounging, it occurred
    To you to draw the pretty bridge

We after crossed; and crossing, saw
    The gay kingfisher bend his flight
Beneath the arch—but could you draw
    The flashing of his azure light?

Then up the winding race we stept;
    The mill-dam's roaring nearer grew,
And shook the lily cups that kept
    Beneath the shade the last night's dew.

Shall we go in? The sun is high,
    And noonday glows on every wave;
The trout refuse the offered fly,
    Whose hues seem more than nature gave.

We enter—twenty windows here
   Light up a room, where nimble hands
Of busy girls, throughout the year,
   Cut dusty rags to cleaner strands.

Perpetual task.  But theirs the power
   To draw the moral of the day,
If haply in an idle hour
   Their fancies ever look that way.

For here and every day is seen
   How Nelson's sails, Napoleon's flags,
The monarch's cloak, the robe of queens,
   All come at last to dusty rags.

And as we look, the opening bale
   Reveals the treasures of the bride,
Who haply sailed a pleasure sail,
   Upon the Adriatic tide

Ten years ago.  The tattered gown
   Of some rude peasant now reposes
Beside the nuptial veil, and one
   Rough sack the union strange incloses!

But now we breathe a purer air,
   Where round the humming engines go,
And in their seething bosoms bear
   The whitening pulp, revolving slow.

Pure is the mass we lately thought
   Was past beyond all human aid;
The city's outcast, hither brought,
   How clean, and white, and fair 'tis made!

And now the endless sheet begins
   Above the cylinders to roll,
And now beneath; while, busy, spins
   The spiral knife that cuts the whole.

And so it is in human life:
   We seem to have an endless flow
Of ups and downs—a hidden knife
   Is always turning round below!

And if our race be short or long,
   The end is sure to be the same;
And none was ever known so strong,
   Could turn the edge when round it came.

And now the wagon bears away
    A load of spotless paper sheets,
To where the Press, by night and day,
    Fills the town air with measured beats.

What varied destiny is theirs—
    The Poet's song; the Lawyer's plea;
The Last Romance; the World's affairs
    That yesternight came o'er the sea.

But look! The shadow of the cone
    Glooms eastward from Monadnoc high,
And soon the captive trout shall own
    That we have deftly wove the fly.

# EPIGRAMS FROM MARTIAL.

### EPITAPHIUM PARIDIS.

TRAVELER, pause.  This Funeral-stone,
From the road you gaze upon,
Pass not in haste.  The joys of Rome,
Egypt's Wit and Song and Pleasure,
Grace and Art, beneath this Dome
Lie—a lost and buried treasure.
No more the theatre's acclaim
Shall stir his heart, locked fast in Death's chill
    keeping.
The Loves and Cupids in the same
Dark tomb with Paris are forever sleeping.

### AD SEXTUM.

YOU say you're not in debt—and 'faith that's true:
They only owe, whom 'tis worth while to sue.

### AD SABIDIUM.

Sabidius, I do not love thee—
Why I don't, I cannot tell;
Only this I know quite well,
That I do not, cannot, love thee!

---

### AD PUELLAM.

Now coy, now bold, now full of fun,
Buz, buz, you fly about me;
I can't live with you—but I've begun,
And now I can't live without thee.

---

### AD ÆMILIANUM.

Æmilianus, if you now are poor,
   You always will be so;
For only to the rich, from Fortune's door,
   Do riches flow.

### IN VARUM.

Varus asked me once to dine—
Splendid glass but scanty wine;
Tables wrought of solid gold;
One small joint, and that was cold—
Every thing to please the eye,
And—to keep one's palate dry.
Next time, Varus, that we meet,
Give me something fit to eat,
Or I'll excuse you from the treat.

### IN PESSIMOS CONJUGES.

This husband and wife are a quarrelsome pair,
And here is the wonder that makes one stare:
  Both alike as any twin pea—
  Both as bad as bad can be—
Isn't it strange they can't better agree?

## ORION.

To-night supreme Orion rules the sphere,
    Lord of the burning Heavens that round him roll;
A giant, resolute and void of fear,
    Spurning the Austral pole,

He strides the firm equator ; 'mid the march
    Of errant, fickle suns, he shows no change,
But in the summit of th' eternal arch
    He runs his constant range.

Around the Boreal pole, the laggard Wain
    Turns its slow wheels for ever to the sight,
And southern stars but rise to hide again
    Their transitory light.

But he, the king of suns, divides the year,
    And half he beams upon the northern world,
And half upon the south ; when leaves are sere,
    In Autumn tempests whirled,

He rises still and stately in the frost,
    That follows hard upon the sinking sun,
And hushes all the gales that lately tossed
    The seas, and forests brown.

In the moist fragrance of the August morn,
    When all the senses fail with summer heat,
Ere yet the fever of the day is born,
    He strides with jeweled feet

Over the mountains of the East, and cries:
    Have courage, O ye fainting sons of men!
Soon will I come, and then the summer dies:
    Soon will I come again,

And bring the sparkle of the Northern snow,
    The airs that stir with pleasure every vein;
When late October winds begin to blow,
    Then will I come again,

And fire the dark of swiftly lengthening nights,
    When once the Hyades have spent their storm,
With belted brilliancy of ruddy lights
    Enwreathed around my form.

Me close shall follow the untiring Hound,
  His head the brightest jewel of the sky;
And me, his lesser mate, with tardy bound,
  Shall chase unceasingly,

Unseen by me. My steadfast eyes are fixed
  On the great Taurus. I a deadly blow
With glittering club eternally present
  Against his shaggèd brow.

The Lion's tawny skin is on my arm,
  My sword hangs glistening at my greavèd knee;
I joy in war, and battle's dread alarm—
  No power can vanquish me.

## H. C. H.

Friend, guileless, tender-hearted, gone before
Through Death's drear gates : I mourn, and mourn
    thee not.
Life's pains and sorrows vex thy soul no more,
And fair thy record shows, and free from spot.
Who dies as thou, is happy : but to live
So purely, merited such length of days
As the kind Heavens oft to mortals give,
Who ripen in their children's children's praise.

## SIR WALTER.

The portrait hangs within the hall,
    Beyond the oaken door,
Upon the black and mouldy wall,
    A yard above the floor.

The hall is damp, and chill, and drear,
    And opens to the ground;
And as you walk therein, you hear
    A dead sepulchral sound.

In former times, its length throughout
    Was choked with dying men,
When savage Walter led the rout,
    And thundered down the glen.

Long since. For now the moat's slow wave
    Smiles to the noonday sun,
Nor shows the corpses of the brave
    Who in its depths were thrown.

By night, the heavy door is drawn,
    The castle stands alone ;
But in the chambers till the dawn
    Unquiet spirits moan.

By day, the slanting sunbeams chase
    Each other through the hall;
But ever on Sir Walter's face
    The gloomy shadows fall.

## ANTI-ARCADIAN.

When Poet's rhymes begin to flag,
    And Pegasus grows crusty;
When appetite is fiercely keen,
    And thought is strangely rusty
Kind Providence an opening leaves
    To save each hungry sinner,
The poet sings a Country-Life,
    And, singing, earns his dinner.


For ever, since old Horace lived,
    And framed the vinous ditty,
Poets of every age and stamp
    Have joined to curse the city:
To curse its noise, its dust, its streets,
    Its artificial gases,
To sigh for pure Arcadian joys,
    And blooming simple lasses.

Such are the rhymes and such the strains
  That take the place of reason—
But as the oyster of July
  Is slightly out of season,
So to my humble sense seems all
  The brood of boundless praises
Of shepherdesses, swains, and maids,
  Of grasses, trees, and daisies.


I don't deny that grass is green,
  That brooks are clear as amber,
That ancient ivies, rich as old,
  O'er mossy oak-trees clamber;
That Beauty meets us everywhere,
  In Nature lights—and shading—
In gardens flushed with wanton Spring—
  In Autumn's foliage fading.


But grass and brooks, and ivies rich,
  Though not a poet's fiction—
What is their value but to aid
  The poet's swelling diction?

ANTI-ARCADIAN.

The veil of beauty hanging round
   Yon distant tranquil cottage—
The inmates find it little worth
   To make—or season—pottage.

Your friend who loves the country much,
   Has bought a *Far Niente*,
And asks you out, in August heats,
   To pass ten days or twenty.
You think it vastly fine to see
   The country in its glory,
And so you pack your rod and gun,
   And throw aside your "Story."

Your friend is very kind, his spouse
   More careful than a mother;
They put you in a feather-bed,
   And leave you there to smother.
The window-sash is battened down,
   The chinks are stuffed with cotton;
Their care has left no single mode
   Of torture unforgotten.

You dream all night of Ætna's fires,
   Of fiendish noises ringing;

You wake—around your hapless face
   You hear mosquitoes singing.
You stagger to the looking-glass—
   Your swollen optics show you,
That even in your father's halls,
   Your sisters wouldn't know you.

You shoot no game—the grounds were cleared
   Last spring by poaching sinners;
The trout refuse your English flies,
   The pickerel scorn your minnows;
The fair, of whom so much was said,
   Have shocking bad complexions;
You shudder at their dentists' bills—
   One has such strange reflections!

No! give to tillers of the field
   Your sympathizing pity;
And praise the country, if you will,
   But keep within the city.
Or if your doctor should advise
   A change of situation,
Select your rural residence
   Hard by a railway station.

## MARGARITA SPOLIATRIX.

**THESE FLED IN 1852, AND WERE LOST AT SEA.**

Why cannot I forget
That I have known you?  Loss of years
Were cheap to purchase Lethe.  Now with tears
To-night my eyes are wet,
And all a vain and fruitless grief:
I hope not—dare not hope—relief.
To-night, what parts us?  House and street;
Naught else.  The rapid feet
Of the chance passer-by, that now I hear,
Will bear him by your door,
Before the foot-fall dies from off my ear:
Yet have the Heavens declared the distance more
Than seas whereof no sailor knows the shore.

What keeps me from your side, you know;
My passion, since it first began to flow,

You largely have divined.  No glance, no sigh,
Has once escaped you.  And you knew that I
Was from the first
Another's: yet you nursed
The flame your presence kindled; seemed to say,
I am the one you should obey,
And false is every other.  Life's mistake
You have committed; but you yet shall break
The chains that now your passion bind,
And happiness with me shall find.
But you have nothing spoken—
Your mystic silence never has been broken;
And pure as yet before the world we stand,
As if we had not neared the fiery strand
Of that vexed ocean, where, when launched our bark,
We sail from God's clear light to unknown wastes of Dark.

Your pitying eyes for ever on me bend,
O less than spoken lover, more than friend !
And if I read them right,
As now my fancy calls me up their light,

They say, When comes the bolder hour,
And Love asserts, at last, its power,
Oh! haste at once to me; for you I wait,
For you I watch, O monarch of my fate!
As I of yours.  O noble soul!
Well have you shown that you can love control.
But why for ever waste the will and nerve
On that dear foe?  Rather does he deserve
That now you yield to him, and prove
The mercy and the sweet rewards of Love.
Ah! silent, pitying eyes—they burn
Through all my sense.  They turn
Always on me; and through them all your being
Mingles with mine, as if, foreseeing
The end of all, you would anticipate
Our destined and inseparable fate.

Often I try
Your charmèd sphere to fly:
I penetrate, I share, the most of all
That can the senses or the mind enthrall—
Places where Pleasure fills its fullest cup,
And royally persuades to drink it up.

But on the waves of music you are borne;
And when the throbbing waltzes mourn,
And bear me circling with the revel's queen,
Your dearer image glides between,
And takes her place. The flashing wine
That lights my soul, is but your smile divine:
The song of morning bird
Becomes your song as soon as heard:
You speak to me
From the warm lispings of the summer sea:
Ah! true
That I must lose myself, ere I lose you!

I come: whatever waits
Of Punishment behind the hidden gates
Where lurks Hereafter—all
I risk, and follow those sweet sounds that call
To where you are. Oh! separated far,
From me if creeds and law's grim duties bar,
For you I all despise—and you are near—
And lo, at once beside you I appear,
Nor more to leave you. With the morn
Shall come astonishment and scorn,

Reproach, and drawing off of friends,
The murmurs of the town,
That every one so quickly lends
To drag his neighbor down.
And shall we care for these—can shame
Attack us, wrapped in Love's bright flame?
Can clamor reach us, sailing far away
Where Nature wantons in a sunnier day,
And brighter stars illume a softer night?
Not thus shall us affright
Our silly fears.  Your hand
I take in mine: at Love's command
We leave the world behind us.  Never more
Its laws shall bear on us as once they bore;
For liberty we barter bonds.  The change
Hath left us free to love and range.
Who shall resist when Fate and Love combine
To press the fragrant wine,
Which now we drink together—sinking there
Of all but Love the consequence and care?

## HARTFORD.

No fairer city in your dreams
   Than ancient Hartford; well you know
The confluence of the silver streams,
   The greater and the lesser flow.
Southward the meadowed Rivers bend,
   Till meads and streams are lost to view;
To east and west the hills extend
   Their forest glens and caps of blue.
Up the long street, the frequent spire
   Fills all the air with tapering lines;
And red by night, the factory fire
   Broad o'er the sleeping country shines.

## NEW ENGLAND HOUSES.

### I.

WHERE winds the river slow away,
    And lingers long at every bend,
And urban gardens, flushed with May,
    Begin with copse and farm to blend,
A House appeared of goodly size,
    And modeled on an ancient plan,
That ARCHITECTUS would despise,
    Whose creed is, Not the house for man,
But man for house; whence crudely grow
    Those miracles of brick and stone,
Which you and I have cause to know,
    Though richer if we had not known.
Before the House the meadows swept,
    In rich unbroken green arrayed,
Till up the distant hills they crept,
    And vanished in the forest shade;
And sitting in the Oriel light
    When first the morning splendor broke,
Clear drawn and large upon the sight,
    Loomed the majestic CHARTER OAK.

## II.

Protected by a sloping ridge
    That overlooks the ancient town,
And where, to cross the five-arched bridge,
    The mail-coach daily thundered down,
You saw my Father's House. A lawn,
    Close shaven, lay before the door;
And when the lattices were drawn,
    The turfy carpet met the floor.
Elm trees arose on either side,
    The nurslings of an elder day,
Whose leafy arches, high and wide,
    All summer kept the green of May.
The House five-windowed, of the style
    Of true New England Houses, white,
And mounted with a gable pile
    That earliest caught the morning light,
When o'er the hills it streamed, and I,
    Awakened from a summer sleep,
Snuffed the late roses of July,
    And heard the brooding sparrow cheep.

And rising in the earliest gray
    Of morning, when the house was still,
Through shaded paths I took my way,
    To darkling pools beneath the mill,
Where in the smoothly flowing tide,
    Unbroken by the sleeping wheel,
I watched my floats and angles glide,
    And filled with trout my wicker creel.

## CHILDHOOD.

No mother, but can truly say—
   And mothers' truth surpasses ours—
That Childhood is an April day,
   A sunshine dimmed with frequent showers.
But as we say, in just degree
   As are the fortunes of the Spring,
So will the flowers of Summer be,
   And so its fruits will Autumn bring.
Thus in our youth is hid the seed
   Of all the fruit that we shall bear;
But who so wise that he can read
   The secret of the Human Year

For dim and buried are the laws
   That bind what is, and is to come;
Though nothing comes without a cause,
   Results oft wander far from home.

Though Boy be father to the Man,
　　The Man may differ from the Boy,
As widely as the deepest pain
　　May differ from the highest joy,
And yet be still the same.　The cause
　　Far-dated, who shall hope to find?
And we, unconscious of its laws,
　　Can only wonder, mute and blind.

．

Do you remember all the crowd
　　Of schoolboys, who at early four
Rushed with tumultuous outcry, loud
　　And eager, through the open door,
That seemed the portal of a joy
　　More joyous than we since have known?
What rapture greater to a boy,
　　Than freedom when his task is done?
Well—surely, to remember all,
　　Would far exceed the ancient task;
And why should I the list recall
　　Which neither you nor readers ask?

The most of these have gone, where go
    The shades of those in later days,
Whom once we thought it well to know,
    But having known, we ceased to praise.


We were a rude and hearty band,
    Of recklessness beyond a name;
Yet some there were, would distant stand,
    And our confederacy disclaim :
The polished gentlemen of ten,
    Who scorned a marble or a ball,
Whose characters contracted stain,
    If e'er they stooped to play at all.
These were the beaux. In old romance
    No cavaliers so grand as these;
No Romeo in tights, that haunts
    The Window at the East, could please
Or flatter with that skilled address
    Which these unbearded knights displayed,
Who never failed of full success,
    No matter where the siege was laid.

Why praise the rough and careless youth,
    The Boy, uncurbed and unpolite?
Because in him th' eternal truth
    Of Nature stands revealed to light.
From out the rough and clodded earth,
    All life and fruits and flowers grow,
A contrast, from their very birth,
    To the dark source from which they flow.
A perfect manhood is a flower,
    That oft from gnarlèd branches shoots;
Nor does the splendor lose its power,
    Because 'twas drawn from earthy roots.
I reverence with faith sincere
    The plan of Him who made us all;
Who makes the Boy devoid of fear,
    And shapes him rough, and fierce and tall;
Implants within his growing frame
    A heart that scorns a smooth pretense,
And stirs in him a quenchless flame,
    That shines through all his active sense.

Unconscious of a future day,
    Of all the cares of after-years,

He revels wide and large in play,
   And careless of all good appears.
Unconscious of his high desert,
   He frets at every curbing rein;
No order he would not subvert,
   No penalty he'd not disdain.
But such make manly men. The flower
   That blooms too soon, or falsely blooms,
Blooms but to wither in an hour,
   While hardier stocks their full perfumes
Keep back at first, until, the sun
   Of Summer kindling into glow
Their opening petals, one by one
   The roses in perfection blow.

## COLLEGE.

I trod the worn Collegiate Halls
  With much of reverence : not in vain
Does Wisdom write upon her walls,
  Far off, ye thoughtless and profane!
For here as in the armory
  Of Palace Beautiful, the sword
And shield and spear are welcome free
  To those alone who love the word
That Wisdom teaches.  Arms like these,
  Immortal and of proof thrice tried,
Let him not rashly hope to seize
  Who wears the flimsy clothes of pride.
Here dwells the air of studious thought;
  In these sequestered shades we see
How from the Past is ever brought
  The hope of Immortality.
Here, in the present moment, we,
  Rejoicing in the influence cast
About our living destiny
  By memories of souls long past,

In the same breath look forward to
    The times to which our souls shall come,
Borne on soft gales that ever blow
    From where the dead have made their home.


Examinations passed, the grave
    Professors reckoned up the score,
How many in the port were safe,
    How many wrecked along the shore.
"From dangers of the wind and tide,
    Deliver us," the mariner prays;
Let kindly Fate for those provide
    Who venture forth for college bays.
Ah! village mother, racked with fear
    When to the trial her Hopeful goes,
But only trembles lest her dear
    May not unbosom all he knows,
*Non cuivis homini*—but stay,
    You don't know Latin—nor did he :
Such was the sentence of the day,
    In which we, sorrowful, must agree.

I love the student—love the years
  That shape the boy into the man;
To me it more and more appears,
  They should be happy as they can.
And when I rule and sway the State—
  Have you no idle dreams like this?—
Each youth, and maiden too, shall wait
  Full age, before their spring-like bliss
Is broken by the weight of care,
  We all must carry: if delayed,
Our manhood's back is strong to bear
  The burden: earlier, overweighed.
And therefore I the more condole
  With those whom Labor early finds,
And trampling on the tender soul,
  In harsh compulsory fetters binds.
Respect them, you who are the more,
  And higher, favored: and if they
To your pre-eminence after soar,
  Cast academic pride away,
And welcome them. The honest guild
  Is always friendly; and the claims
That on a badge or ribbon build,
  Are at the best but glittering shames.

O Friend! who, eddying here and there,
    Still love o'er olden days to dream,
And now far off are listening, where
    Rolls Sacramento's golden stream;
What days were ours, when, classic-full—
    With mathematics saturate—
For the nonce we voted Plato dull,
    And Parallelopipedons vowed to hate!
Sad disrespect! But who shall blame
    Those hours passed in rosy mirth?
Unless—the Gods avert the same—
    Those musty Greeks return to earth.


Where now is dear old Tutor Blank,
    Who, stunned by our Round-Table glees,
Would creep to the door, and softly, "Thank
    You Gentlemen all, and—milder, please."
Then down the stairs again, good soul,
    Obliged to vindicate the laws,
Yet knowing that his mild control
    Was hailed through College with applause;

While those who envied us our mirth,
  And harried all our nights, were coaled,
Gunpowdered to the very hearth,
  And waked by bells untimely tolled.

---

As for the suppers—not to swerve
  From truth in any just degree,
I cannot say that they deserve
  That they should much be praised by me:
At raw sixteen, or ere of age,
  The gust, insatiable and crude,
Incites the palate to engage
  With things unknown to Monsieur Ude.
At best, the Science scarcely known
  On this our hemisphere as yet,
Was but to scant proportions grown
  Among the folk of Quodlibet.
And if with these so slender, worse
  With the Publicans—who ever are
With sinners coupled, as of course
  Including these, and much to spare.

The wise arch enemy of youth,
   Attacking them in every part,
Assaults—there's no profounder truth—
   The stomach, equally with the heart.
For with a diabolic sleight,
   Persuading them that youthful sense
And flush of youthful appetite
   Are of enduring permanence,
They rush to strange repasts, combine
   All elements of peptic woe,
Dilute with fearful brands of wine,
   The child of vitriol and sloe.
Hence comes with sure and swiftest pace,
   A fiend, the progeny of Hell,
And he, who once has seen his face,
   Needs not that I his name should tell.
Dyspepsia call him, that the few
   Who live remote from earthly cooks,
May share that faint innoxious view
   One gets of vicious things in books.
Once seized by those remorseless hands,
   All struggles are but fruitless pain;
He grasps securely, and the bands
   He twists are proof to mental strain.

What hope remains to stir the soul,
    Mocked by this devil foul and mean,
Who o'er the mansion holds control,
    And lets no peace or sunshine in?

---

O Friend! who in a sunnier land,
    But not on sunnier duties bent,
By sealed Executive command,
    Doth judge a Georgia settlement,
And skilled in Blackstone and the Law,
    As highest taught, doth yet descend
To parley with the lamest saw
    Of rustic justices, and blend
Thy loftier wisdom with the wit
    Of shallow lawyers from the town,
Who, since they cannot fathom it,
    Miscalculate its true renown:
Do yet your thoughts return with mine
    To college times, when in the shade
Of summer nights and whispering pine,
    We sonneteered th' unconscious maid?

When, underneath the mighty arch
    Where hung the moon's resplendent horn,
And gazing on the ceaseless march
    Of Scorpio and Capricorn,
Great thoughts possessed our souls, and we—
    Though dimly we suspected then,
That they with stars and night would flee,
    And leave us desolate again—
Loved none the less the pleasing spell
    That held us in its drowsy arms:
Night and soft airs uniting well
    Their fragrant, rare, Nepenthean charms?


But chief among the trooping joys
    That gleamed in Fancy's marshalled host,
And marched with steadiest equipoise,
    And claimed our hearts' dear reverence most,
Was Love—not clearly drawn his shape,
    Nor all revealed, as when the form
Of some high, memorable Cape,
    Faint glistens through a sunlit storm,

Well known, but only from the chart,
   And hailed as guide to tranquil seas;
So Love seemed ancient to the heart,
   But only from its histories.
We worshiped each, an unknown maid,
   Some congeries of beauties rare,
Whose worth of fame a bankrupt made,
   And kind, we hoped, as she was fair.
Around this image, Love decreed
   That all should worship, chiefly we.
How easy were it to succeed,
   If worship were the guarantee!
No worship of our later days,
   In actual lady's actual bower,
Did more the heart's emotions raise,
   Or flatter Love with greater power,
Than ours in college days, unknown
   To aught but us—unknown the shrine—
If shrine there were—a strange, vague tone
   Of music from a source divine!

# EPIGRAMS FROM MARTIAL.

### AD FLACCUM.

FLACCUS, you ask me why I love at all;
   Or why, if loving, I retain a part
Of my soul's wealth? What, shall a girl enthrall
   Supremely and forever Martial's heart?
No. I would not surrender my estate
   In my own self—nor yet too niggard be:
On female pity let me never wait,
   Nor treat the maid with harsh severity.
Safe is the middle course. My joyous breast
   Shall love and live, and live in willing love;
No jealous sorrows shall disturb its rest,
   Nor shall it sigh for maids who cruel prove.

### AD FABULLAM.

FABULLA, when you swear
That this is your own hair
Which you, so jaunty, wear,
Some say you perjured are;
But I deny it:
As for the slander, I defy it;
It *is* your hair—I saw you buy it!

---

### AD LESBIAM.

GIVE me kisses, sweetest maid:
What! "How many?" have you said?
 Bid me count the ocean waves,
  Or shells that the Ægean sea
 Casts on the shores it kindly laves
  From Argos round to Thessaly;
 Bid me count the bees that fly
  Round the Cecropian mountains high:
 He deserves but kisses few,
  Who calculates their number, too.

## DE DIAULO MEDICO.

Diaulus lately was a Quack,
　　Now he is an Undertaker;
'Tis but going one step back :
Those whom once he killed, as Quack,
　　Now he hides with Mother Nature.

---

## AD PUELLAM.

Jane wants to marry Thomas—that's not bad :
　　If she could only get him, 'twould be stunning;
But *he* refuses—he's a knowing lad,
　　And cleverer than she takes him for—at running.

## THE POET'S PRAYER.

#### HORACE, ODE XXXI. BOOK I.

What asks the Poet at Apollo's shrine,
   When first he dedicates his votive hymn;
When with proud heart he pours the sacred wine
   From the wide goblet's brim?


Not the fat harvests of Calabrian grain,
   Nor flocks that crop the green Sicilian wold;
Not gleaming ivory from the Indian plain,
   Nor world-alluring gold.


Let the gay vintager, 'neath sunny skies,
   Trim the rich clusters of Burgundian vine:
From golden beakers, bought with Tyrian dyes,
   Let merchants quaff their wine—

Dear to the Gods: for thrice within the year
   Their ships have passed th' Herculean columns
      high,
Which, girt with waves, and storms that stun the
      ear,
   Frown on the Atlantic sky.


All these I ask not: let me only see
   My board with grapes and olives humbly spread
And for a rarer dessert, let there be
   The mallow's tender head.


Thus, Great Apollo, speed my happy days:
   Let healthy mind in healthy body dwell;
Nor to my waning years be wanting praise,
   Nor music's soothing spell.

## THE MILL-WHEEL.

Within the mill-wheel's dripping cave,
   How flies the white and gleaming spray,
In music falling on the wave
   That dances to the open day!
How cool the eddies of the stream,
   In lazy beats returning slow
About the black and roughened beam,
   Whose mossy feet are far below!

The mill above is racked with noise,
   And gray with clouds that ever fly;
And now I hear the miller's voice,
   As here and there the workmen ply.
I hear the wagons at the door,
   The din of bargain in the hall;
The wheel beneath the raftered floor
   Groans on, the willing slave of all:

## THE MILL-WHEEL.

Unheedful of the summer wind
   That o'er the rippling water skims;
Unheedful of the frosts that bind
   With icy blades its dripping rims;
Nor ever slacks its measured sound,
   To think of all it has to do,
But patient turns its endless round,
   As if its will were endless too.

By night the water-gate is drawn,
   Beneath the wave the wheel is still;
And waiting for the ling'ring dawn,
   In silence stands the lonely mill.
Sleep, busy wheel—a respite ask
   When all thy daily work is done;
And would the morn's recurring task
   Were less the image of my own.

# HINTS FROM THE SIXTH SATIRE

When now the Dog-Star lit the morning sky,
And grapes were red, and autumn hours were nigh,
And long vacation, hastening to a close,
Endeared each August sun that loitering rose;
We mused away a shady afternoon,
Dreaming the Future that would meet us soon;
From this to that we wandered, passing o'er
Wide tracts of hope, and fame, and love, and lore,
With easy, careless flight. Ah! bliss of youth,
Ere care and sorrow bring unwelcome truth.
And I, scholastic biased, praised a life
Lone, celibate, and far from worldly strife.
But then Horatio laughed: "A foolish dream!
Let but a maiden's eyes upon you beam,
And where's your frost-work?" "Let the sage declare,"
I said, " if we must, slavish, serve the fair—
Not so have I perused the lives of men
Of whom we say, ' They have not lived in vain.'

Nay, from all records, easy 'tis to prove
That Genius has no heavier clog than Love."

"O, rebel to your father's faith and deeds!
If such crude heresies your learning breeds,
I cast away the ancient musty saws,
And Love and Nature shall enforce their laws."

"*Macte virtute*, O my friend!" I said,
"Let me read you what I myself have read;
Nor dare despise the wisdom of the bard,
Though you may hold my verse in slight regard.
To your condition I adapt the strain,
And hymn Horatio in the 'Ercles' vein."
"If I may yawn or sleep," he said, "agreed."
"Agreed," said I. "Then, worst of poets, read!"

Once, I believe, on this degenerate earth,
Virtue, and laws, and morals, had their birth;
When the cold grotto and the mountain cave
A resting-place to flock and shepherd gave;
When, on the skins of bears and lions spread,
The rustic mother made her children's bed.

A simple soul, unlike that Roman fair,
Who mourned dead sparrows to a plaintive air;—
Uncouth and rough, her progeny attest
The strength they drew from her abundant breast.
For when the earth and when the heavens were new,
A giant race of men from giants grew.
Peaceful and strong, they tilled the joyous earth,
And Nature blessed the homes that gave them birth.

Such was the golden age: the silver came,
And brought the god of fond Danäe's flame:
No cot too lowly to be safe from Jove,
No maid unnoticed by his lawless love.
Then fled Astræa! then no longer lay
Fair mansions open to the public way:
Trembling, the rustic feared licentious art,
And safe no longer was the virgin's heart.

Old is the custom, nor improved by age,
With lying fraud the female heart to gauge,
Try all its weaker points, and shrewdly mine
Just where self-love and love for you combine.

## HINTS FROM THE SIXTH SATIRE. 85

But woman in the brazen age began
To wreak revenge upon inconstant man.
Whatever ills our present time may bring,
A faithless woman is no modern thing:
Fruit of our craft, perverted by our art,
She triumphs newly in each broken heart.

Yet, my Horatio, by the world 'tis said,
You have, though young, made up your mind to wed.
The presents and the contracts are prepared,
Nor are your tailor or your barber spared.
It is your ring that sparkles to the day,
When the fair Julia promenades Broadway.

Oh! woman's wiles, that could a Samson bind—
Is this Horatio, once so strong of mind?
What, when the hempen cord the neck invites,
When sly garroters fill our streets o' nights;
When from your window high, an easy cast
Will make your flight your longest and your last;
Nay, when the Staten Island ferry shows
So sure an ending of all human woes—

Why choose a fate, a fate unending, too,
That wise men shun?—but these, alas! are few.

The college says, no bachelor's retreat
Vies with Horatio's—so exact and neat.
No woman's wars its owner's rest surprise—
*Procul profanæ*, meets all female eyes;
A well-clad Jenkins spreads the quiet roast—
Jenkins, your marriage will amaze the most:
Nor count it strange that wonder seize us all,
If in a female net, Horatio fall.

O wondrous being, that can thus enchain
The haughty spurner of the female rein!
Let votive thanks proclaim your new-found joy,
And garlands offer to the Archer Boy.
Oh! who is Julia? Are her conquests few,
That she, so young in years, has fixed on you?
Or, do a hundred rapt companions share
In those love-tokens you so gayly wear?
Can you aver yourself the only one
On whom your Julia's eyes have fondly shone?
I know a girl, who lives at home, afar,
Where the blue Catskill cleaves the upper air;

Distant her father's house, and lone the spot,
The tax-collector scarcely knows the route;
Yet twenty lovers ken the devious road
That often guides them to her sire's abode.
If "each is able who believes he can,"
Then, on my faith, is each the happy man.

O wise Horatio! can the town e'er show
A wife devoted to your fate and you?
I grant, in wit and manly sense you shine—
But can you troll the sentimental line?
Or do you catch each last-imported air,
Where ballet-girls display, and foot-lights glare?
Say, can you match your rivals in the dance—
Like them can you direct the tender glance,
When the soft motions of the reeling waltz
Bring cheek to cheek, and fire the bounding pulse?
Like Roscius, simulate a Hamlet's frown,
Or, a young Romeo, drink the midnight down?
Dullest of mortals—can you hope to please,
Who cannot act, or sing, or dance like these?
If, a grave judge, you try the censor's art,
You'll find the ladies do not like the part;

When in May Fair the gay Bathyllus dines,
The sage Quinctilian in his garret pines.


But grant the ring, and grant the contract too,
Will the fair Julia to yourself be true?
Straight to the altar will she take her way,
When patient waiting brings the expected day?
Oh! who can count the fancies, passion-bred,
That now, as ever, turn the female head!
Does rank, or wit, or fashion ever pall?
Yes: Fancy reigns supreme, and laughs at all.


To sultry Egypt, says the ancient rhyme,
Came the fair Hippia—fairest of her time:
On Rome's broad avenues, her father's gate
Stood open only to the rich and great.
There did she wed a senator and lord,
Who loved, as Romans loved, who kept their word.
But, fatal day! a gladiator came,
And changed the current of her life and fame:
Terrific Giant! with a single hand
He threw the panting leopard on the sand;

The fierce Numidian lion, human-fed,
First from that awful frown abjectly fled,
Confessed his conqueror while he coursed the ring,
And died, forgetful of his deadly spring.
But bloodier deeds the populace admired;
And who like Sergius, when of beasts they tired?
When thumbs went up around the Ædile's stand,
And hundreds dropped before his murderous brand,
Survivor sole, the dauntless man of blood,
Panting with slaughter, in the circus stood;
Perceived those lustrous eyes that on him turn—
Ah! matchless eyes that could so deeply burn!
Noble Fabricius, at the Forum stay,
Strength and the sword have lured thy bride away.
Where Pharos glows, and warm Egyptian air
Stirs the slow Nile, have fled the raptured pair;
Daring the treacherous winds and angry sea,
Fled from the games, the baths, and least—from thee!

Long dead is Hippia—but every day
Repeats, and will repeat, the ancient lay:
Oh! why did Helen win a deathless fame,
A fame whose lustre gilds the brow of shame?

Why gleams so long the sad enduring light
Of this fair sinner, robed in legend bright?
Yet hearts are tender: passion's throbs are strong,
And jealous husbands always in the wrong.
Avoid, rash man, to use a husband's power,
When the gay tempter first invades thy bower;
Nor fear that from your side your wife will stray,
Unless your negligence prepare the way.
To every wily, every flattering art,
Oppose the kindness of a loving heart:
Revive the soft attentions you displayed,
When first you wooed the coy and bashful maid.
Think not a woman can forget the charm
Of the soft whisper and the willing arm;
If you withhold these tributes of your love,
And hope with rugged threats her heart to move,
Blame not your fate, nor woman's faith despise,
If to another, Heaven transfer the prize.

But justly blame the foolish wretch who made
His wife the venture of a sordid trade;
Who bought consent with money counted down,
And bribed a rustic with a house in town.

On legal parchment were the contracts drawn,
The vows were registered by priests in lawn;
A cringing father gave the bride away,
A scheming mother blessed the golden day;
The spreading news provokes the jealous smart,
And baleful envy fires each rival's heart.
But when did age and money e'er control
The quick emotions of the female soul?
Too soon the dastard lost his feeble hold
Upon the woman purchased by his gold;
While his weak limbs compel unwilling rest,
She lights the torches and prepares the feast;
She fills the cups, and twines the garlands gay,
Bids through the halls the nimble dancers play,
And prompts the revels till the dawn of day.
Nor does she force the miser's heart alone
O'er costly feasts and wasted wine to groan:
With jealous pangs she poisons all his life,
Till death release him from his pains, and wife!

Such pensive tales of matrimonial woe
Shall surely meet you whereso'er you go;
And if the mention should your taste offend,
Blame not the humble bard, but them, my friend.

But grant your Julia good, and fair, and true,
Say that she venerates her sire and you;
Let her be fonder than the Sabine band
Who brought fair peace to all the Roman land;
In fine, a *rara avis*—such a bird
As sweetly singing, you nor I have heard:
Yet with all this, and with much more beside,
The deadly bane of all her charms is Pride.

Oh! woman's pride! I'd rather wed a slave
Than thee, Cornelia, mother of the brave,
If with your virtues and your wealth you bring
Those cursed airs that from such dower spring!
Oh! take away those legends of your race:
How your great grandsire held the Premier's place;
How, with applauding voice, the state conspires
To sound the praises of your line of sires.
Let this suffice—if e'er the marriage state
I rashly enter, spare me such a mate!

Who is not wiser than th' egregious fool
Who takes a wife from out a modern school,
Where female souls o'er Greek and Latin dream,
And Ologies are bolted by the ream?

Will Greek compound a dessert or a pie,
Or half-learned Latin aid in housewifery?
And yet these noble tongues, if understood,
Commend themselves to all the wise and good.
But the pert Miss disdains the studious line,
Contented she in smatterings to shine;
But shines so ill, your only thought is this—
If such be knowledge, ignorance is bliss!

Short is the maxim, but 'tis full of weight—
Than wives, the good deserve a better fate.
Submit your head, and let your neck prepare
The yoke of your ambitious spouse to wear,
And while you yield, your wife will never spare:
Quick, at her word, you send the poor away;
You pass a bargain, if she thunder nay;
Your trusty college chum—your dearest friend—
She to the right-about will boldly send.
She now will guide your taste—your bosom's lord,
She tunes your voice, and modulates each word;
This shall you like—not that; this friend shall shun,
And with a shilling cut your favorite son.

These are hard burdens—harder you endure,
If your dear spouse affect the foreign tour;
No Eastern queen was ever half so grand,
Or had so fond a slave at her command.
But still obey—and still you'll find it true,
That if you marry, you'll have work to do.

Start not, Horatio! but be firm and bold,
While I the source of greater woes unfold:
Mothers-in-Law I sing—a baleful race,
Who leave no concord where they find a place;
Who know no pity—no forbearance know,
But o'er the ruins of a houschold grow;
But let it partly for their acts atone,
That, at the worst, your wife can bring but one!

Despair of slippered quiet while she lives,
Or goods secure: for on your spoil she thrives.
Deep in your tradesmen's books she finds a place,
And swells your Christmas bills with easy grace:
"These comforts, while my daugher lasts, she needs,
Poor wretch, o'er whom a mother's bosom bleeds!

Once she was young and happy, gay and fair;
Now, mark her altered face and languid air:
Slave to your whims, she wastes her life away,
And Death too soon will seize his easy prey:
While thus her youthful charms and graces fade,
Dare not to slight the ruin you have made;
Do not remorseless see your victim die:
Yield to her fancy—please her longing eye.
What baseness to begrudge a trifling cost,
When soon you'll mourn the treasure you have lost!"


Surrender, friend, nor tempt th' unequal game—
To fight and not to fight, are both the same.
Perhaps you'll say—and say with justice too—
A dying woman has a deal to do,
And runs up bills as if she died for two.
Thus free your mind, thus vent your wrath in air.
To marry not a woman, but a pair,
Is but the common lot—the common rule,
That binds alike philosopher and fool.

In the good times when George the Fourth was
    king,
The Ladies loved the race-course and the ring;
Lisped dainty oaths, drank healths a finger deep,
And reckoned lightly of a five-barred leap.
And still the ardor of the British dame,
Invades our modern fair with equal flame:
But changed the mode, nor is its course the same;
For now they tempt the sacred preacher's part,
And with learn'd airs essay the healing art;
Burst through the shackles of our narrow code,
And prove that Home is not their true abode.
For thus, when folly-mad, the female soul
Nor loves a home, nor brooks its mild control.
What, shall your spouse a loud haranguer be?
Can she adore at once the crowd and thee?
Then let her habit ape the cut of ours,
Rub from her cheeks those rosy blushing flowers;
Toughen those tender limbs, enforce the gait,
The graces banish that around her wait;
And view the monster calmly, if you can,
The proper scorn of woman and of man.

But why does vain ambition thus invade
Those tender souls, for Love and Duty made?
Why should the fair transgress the silken bond
That would detain them in their graceful round?
Why do they, thoughtless, ally with our foes,
When leagues of follies shake the state's repose?

Once, humble fortune made our women chaste,
Keepers at home, and envious of waste;
Content to be the handmaid of her lord,
Each matron, duteous, spread his humble board;
Cared for his comfort, made his fame her pride,
Nor dreamed beyond her home of aught beside.
While on his lips the state and forum hung,
She for sweet household words reserved her tongue;
Or if with industry and busy care,
He courted Fortune, and she heard his prayer,
She did not waste the rich increasing store,
Nor while he gathered, dissipate the more.

But now we suffer all the thousand woes
That scourge a people sunk in long repose;
For Luxury, more fierce than hostile arms,
Deludes the social realm with baleful charms.

No crime is absent where she rules the state,
And round her throne all deadly vices wait.
She steeps our youth in swift precocious crime,
Before they touch the years of manly prime;
Taints every office that our rulers hold,
And buys up justice with a purse of gold.
If such the truth, if such our manhood grown,
Can you expect the sex to stand alone?
Will woman soar above her spouse or sire?
Or than the fountain, can the stream rise higher?

Bad men are bad; but woman bad is worse:
Such is the law of Nature—such its curse.
What oaths, what shameless passion, when you meet
The reckless harlot in the public street!
This is the dire extreme—but grant it so;
And does it less the course of Nature show?
So true in all, that when the angels fell,
The highest seraph led the van of Hell!
So true in all, that in the subtlest phase
In which the front of life its heart betrays,
The sinning woman sins the worst of all—
If in the least she stumble, she must fall.

Nor dream that soon as wealth and ease begin,
And boundless pleasures teach us how to sin,
That Nature's laws will from their track depart,
Or drive temptation from the female heart;
That then a foreign vice will cease to charm,
Or French philosophy protect from harm.
As o'er the crowned and wealthy Roman state,
When long luxurious Peace had loosed the gate,
Flowed lawless Sybaris, and drunken Rhodes,
And all the license of the Capuan codes;
So now our manners show the foreign stain
That blots the march of commerce and of gain,
And darkest, deepest, worst of all, displays
Where female art the social sceptre sways.

Dismiss your graver cares, and venture out
When some fair sinner gives a midnight rout,
What time the honest world is safe abed,
And peaceful slumber stills each virtuous head.
Then when the horns with brassy tremors sound,
And close-locked pairs in dizzying whirls go round;
When the vexed air a deafening chaos fills,
Until your hearing seems the worst of ills;

When lavish goblets, all too often poured,
In foaming beauty glisten round the board;
When now the reeling house tumultuous swims,
And candles double as the eye-sight dims;
When the kind favors of the hour permit
The farthest license of the dubious wit;
When virgins, bolder than their lovers grown,
Demand an ardor equal to their own—
Then, as the morning pales the waxen glare,
And rising sun-beams pierce the heavy air,
Pick through the noisy crowd your careful way;
And while you taste the freshness of the day,
Lament the milder orgies of the state
That nursed a Louis and his precious mate,
And blame your destiny you live so late.


I know how sagely ancient friends advise
The help of guardians, and of watchful eyes;
Restrain their social follies—keep them in,
Nor let the wandering footstep tempt to sin.
SED QUIS CUSTODIET—you know the rest;
A task ungrateful, difficult at best.

For when the morning stage your bulk conveys
To the dim office where you pass your days,
To whom will you the manly part confide,
Of confidential jailor to your bride?
Or when three courses and your pint of wine
Your nodding brain to slumbers soft incline,
(How vain to strive against the drowsy hour,
If evening papers lend their leaden power!)
Who shall escort your daughter or your spouse,
To play Asmodeus in your neighbor's house?
Nay, should you pension Argus by the year,
And bribe the wistful winds to lend an ear,
Your wife is cunning, doubles their rewards,
And finds her safety in your chosen guards!

In vain would melting words and airs combine,
If Tenors did not sing, or Bassos shine;
For since the Opera has hither flown,
And we can call the lyric stage our own,
Which please the fair the most, 'tis hard to tell—
Italian strains, or those who sing them well.

Ah! mournful truth—how oft the morning sheet
And table-talk their dire results repeat!

Teach your fair daughters, with the strictest rules,
To fly from fortune-hunters and from fools;
To flirt with prudence, and with just degree
To draw the line between the kind and free:
Let learnèd graces lend their costly aids
To gild the charms of these accomplished maids;
Still, naught, and worse than naught, is all this art,
When Loves of Tenors storm the female heart.
A thousand virgins at Edgardo's shrine
Pour their fond sighs, and floral offerings twine;
Nor can the hero's generous feelings bear,
That they should waste their vows on empty air.
Now from the painted lawn, the ochred grove,
His songs responsive whisper love for love;
The melting magic of his tuneful voice
Invites surrender where he rests his choice,
Compels all foes and obstacles to yield,
And leaves Edgardo master of the field;
Then "strange elopement by the midnight train"—
The world's loud laughter, and the mother's pain.

The stage-deluded fair our pity claim,
But fly with hasty fear the wrathful dame,
With brows of iron and with eyes of flame;

Who holds the luckless family in awe,
And boasts where'er she goes, her word is law.
Terrific theme! with careful art control
Your cautious words, nor vex her angry soul;
For, of all woes that scourge our wretched race,
A brawling woman holds the foremost place.

Nor much inferior in the scale of ill
Is she who practises the critic's skill;
Compares the ancient and the modern song,
And tells what faults to this and that belong.
She praises Virgil, but she must aver
That in his figures he was wont to err:
How could Æneas wed the Tyrian queen,
And those long centuries of time between?
Homer she doubts. "In that barbaric night,
It were a question whether bards could write;
The pleasing poems that adorn his name,
And which not wholly undeserve their fame,
Are fruit and product of a later day,
Styled 'Homer' in a sort of jesting way,
As now 'Anonymous' we often say."
Nor less does Shakspeare meet her learned doubt:
Historic fiction of an age gone out;

A tavern-jester, with a forehead high,
Behind whose smooth expanse no brains were known to lie.
'Tis a keen joke: the wits of Shakspeare's time
Made him the post whereon to hang their rhyme:
Then if the verse were praised, they took the praise;
If damned, they asked, "Who writes such shocking plays?"
This game, for Verulam and Raleigh fit,
A pastime exquisite of courtly wit,
Has made us heir to that immortal page
That glows the brighter as it gathers age.
But as in Homer, so in Shakspeare too,
The age it is, and not the man, we view.
The age of heroes and the age of song,
Inscribed by all the minds that through it throng,
Condensed at last within a single name,
That smoothly walks th' eternal road of fame.
Such is the theme at Ladies' lectures read,
The wondrous offspring of a female head;
And backed by logic of such trenchant stuff,
That e'en logicians own 'tis quite enough.

Now let the bard—

     "Desist," Horatio cried,
"Nor write your author dead, and me beside.
Well for your bones, that centuries ago
Your injured poet went where all must go.
What monstrous jumble have you here composed,
Old times and new in one rough shell inclosed?
I pass your dullness, pass your halting rhyme,
The slanderous verse that ill befits the time;
I only ask, desist to ape the sage
Who mourns the follies of his buried age.
In vain the long-drawn martial verse you try,
Your mother's counsels give your muse the lie;
And if love's passion e'er your bosom stirs,
Another's whispers will but strengthen hers."

"The argument *ad hominem*," I cried,
"Your guide, philosopher, and friend—your bride.
But let the public judge between us two,
If I can find a publisher—or you."

## ADVICE.

A CERTAIN preacher asked a friend's advice
About his sermons, for his drowsy flock
Strayed off, or slept, and recked not of the Word.
The critic came, and kept an open ear,
Till in the vestry met, the preacher asked:
"Well, well?"  And he: "With candor I have
  heard,
And your discourse a certain something lacks.
And I suggest, that to recall your fold,
You find some one to write your sermons for you;
And pardon me, if also I advise,
That—then, you get somebody else to read them!"

# EPIGRAMS FROM MARTIAL.

### DE GEMELLO ET MARONILLA.

Gemellus wants to marry Maronilla;
Day and night he hangs about her villa;
Seeks and urges—hastens on the day;
From her side is scarce an hour away;
Lavish gifts on her is ever pressing:
Such devotion—faith, 'tis quite distressing!
Is she handsome? Handsome as a hedge-
Hog; her face would set your teeth on edge;
Stupid, old, and ugly: but her money
Turns the gall of all this dose to honey;
And the sweetest drop is this: her cough
Is sure in twenty weeks to take her off.

### IN CALENUM.

Once your fortune was but small,
Then your home was free to all;
Joyous, gay, and prodigal.
Such a generous host, Calenus,
We, your thousand friends, between us
Wished that Fortune's happy chance

To you her bounties might impart,
And recompense with rich advance
The largess of your liberal heart.
The kindly goddess heard our prayer,
Made you unexpected heir
Of two rich widows, in a day
Snatched from their estates away.

What then? At once your doors you close,
Compel yourself a pauper's woes.
On crusts and wilted lettuce dine,
Washed down with cheap and musty wine.
No longer do you wish a friend,
For fear that you'll be asked to lend.
No longer you enjoy the hour
When wit and mirth assert their power.
Your life is gain; your only joy
Is base, and sordid usury.
But still our prayer to Fortune rises,
That she will grant you fresh surprises;
If she'll but double, treble, your possessings,
You'll starve to death—'twould be the best
    of blessings.

## AD PRISCUM.

You ask me why so late in life
I am a bachelor. My wife
I have not found, as yet; but you, inhuman,
Desire me to wed that wealthy woman
Who has a fancy for me—not to boast;
And sends me billet-doux by every post.
I like her not: she is too proud for me:
A matron, to my mind, should ever be
Less than her husband; only thus we find
The sexes in equality combined.

## AD CATONEM IN THEATRO.

O rigid Judge! already well you know
The secrets of the circus and the show;
The games of mountebanks; the midnight ball;
The maskers' revels—yes, you know them all;
When lo, I meet you in the crowded pit!
But why stand up? 'Tis easier to sit:
Or did you only come through mud and rain,
In order that you might go out again?

## AROOSTOOK.

THE sun is coming from the South,
   I hear the bluebird's cheerful lay;
The river from its loosened mouth
   Pours leagues of crashing ice away.

And this is April. Once I dreamed
   Away a southern happy year,
Where sunbeams through the roses gleamed
   In April. Are there roses here?

What binds the race to Labrador,
   The squalid wastes of Hecla's side,
The Orkneys, and the Norway shore,
   And rocks that front the Polar tide;

To which these piny realms of Maine
   Are gardens? Though the sun invite,
And call me to the South again,
   To tropic air and balmy night,

Yet here I linger—here is Home:
   Its tender spell is round me cast,
Endearing skies of sullen gloom,
   Short summer marred by bitter blast.

## AT MANILLA.

The ship that bore me here at twenty-two,
    Lies underneath the sea;
Nor she, nor other ship that sails the blue,
    To homeward shores shall ever carry me.

If life give little, yet it gives one choice,
    Before we fix our fate:
Be mine, Content. Who seeks for greater joys,
    On him shall sorrows fall with greater weight.

I will not nurture friends to see them die,
    Or watch their love decay;
Nor taste God's dearest gift—a child's sweet cry—
    To be soul-wrecked when that is snatched away.

Within my heart, in soft, perpetual bloom,
    There lives a maiden face,
And all my life her constant smiles illume,
    Nor leave for sadness any resting-place.

The kiss she gave is on my lips to-day,
   Warmed with a balmy sigh;
To-morrow there—nor will it pass away
   So long as I am true to memory.

Though I grow old, yet she will never change—
   Her smile will be as fair.
Shall I return to gaze on features strange,
   And reft by time of charms that once were there?

If Fate hath made us so, that every hour
   She steals away a joy,
Yet this is left, that I escape her power,
   Nor rest my soul on what she may destroy.

# OVID.

### PARIS AD HELENAM.

Daughter of Leda,
               I a greeting send,
The blameless courtesy of friend to friend.
And shall I further speak? What need to tell
Of Love that Helen sees and feels too well?
Alas! too well. Let me the flame repress,
While unsuspected hours our meetings bless.
But lamely I dissemble: how conceal
Fires which their own bright tongues to all reveal?
But if you wait—if you expect the word,
I LOVE, 'tis past recall, and you have heard.
Spare me, love-wearied: let a kindly face
Bend o'er the line that leaves me to your grace.
This boon is great, that you receive the prayer,
Which gathers freshening hope, because you spare.
Because you spare, I bless the Goddess kind,
Who led me here, and taught what I should find.

For hither have I come by her command,
Who, all-victorious, draws with tender hand.
I seek for great rewards: but they are due,
And she, who promised all, has given me You,
And thus fulfilled the compact.

       For the prize
O'er boundless seas I came, to where arise
The Isles Ægean. She, complaisant airs
Breathed from the skies in answer to my prayers.
The sea-sprung Goddess, who commands the sea,
Smoothed all its waves, that I might come to thee.

Love's flames I brought—I did not find them here;
These fixed my journey—not the stormy year;
Nor chance, nor skillful pilot, is the cause
Why Trojan guest obeys the Spartan laws.
Nor merchant filled my ships with silken bales:
My wealth is Love—with this the Trojan sails.
Nor yet spectator I of Grecian power:
Lord of unbounded wealth, and Love the Dower.
But You I seek—by Venus led, I came,
Worshiped by me before I heard your name;

Clear-lighted to my heart your features shone,
And, first of women, you were loved ere known!

And do you wonder? Has it never been,
That Cupid's bow has wounded, twanged unseen?
So will the Fates—and, not to cross their power,
Hear what befell me at my natal hour.

Unborn I lingered. Long my mother bore
The ripened burden that oppressed her sore;
Till, fever-pulsed, she dreamed that in her lay
A blazing brand, that burned her life away;
Shuddering she rose, and groping 'mid the night
Through the dim palace, stood in Priam's sight;
And told the vision. He, whom Gods inspire,
Foretold in me the red and baleful fire
Cassandra sings for Troy. But far apart
From truth. This firebrand is Paris' Heart;
Incensed with love, its generous embers glow,
The wealth and hope of Troy, and not her foe.

There is a nook within the woody vales
Of Middle Ida, hid from blustering gales
By bosky laurels; oaks and elms on high
Shade the hot noon, but not obscure the sky.

Here, not the timid sheep disturbs the vine,
Nor venturous kid, nor pasture-loving kine,
So devious, dim, the path; and here I came
One summer's day, when all the sky was flame,
And myrtle-shaded sat, and watched the wave,
Whose languid ripples scarce a murmur gave;
And saw far off the white and shining walls
Of rich imperial Troy.
                Then faintly falls
The tread of musically-moving feet,
Whose heavenly rhythms all the glades repeat,
For not of mortal step; and while I feared,
First to my eyes swift Mercury appeared,
Herald of Goddesses, the God; for him
Close followed, threading through the foliage dim,
Minerva, Juno, Venus, stepping light,
On beds of Asphodel and Crocus bright.

Trembling I looked, as one who in amaze,
At midnight wakes, when red Auroras blaze.
But he: "Be not afraid, these leave the sky—
Their golden thrones—a mortal's skill to try,
In Parliament of Beauty: you are he,
O favored one! with whom the choice shall be."

Could I refuse? He spoke the will of Jove,
And, heavenly omen, straightway soared above.
Left to myself, my fainting sense grew strong,
And Jove-inspired, I conned the beauteous throng.
Each worthy seemed to conquer; in the eyes
Of their fond judge, each merited the prize;
But still the fairest, she who most compelled,
Was Love's great mother.

      Nor were gifts withheld
By any—richer than all dreams, and these
But trifling earnests of the boundless fees
From her who was to conquer. Jove's great
 spouse,
Wide kingdoms, and a crown about my brows,
Securely promised; but Minerva's prize,
Statecraft, and all that in clear wisdom lies.
Between the two I paused; till Venus laughed:
"Philosopher nor king the stream has quaffed
That now I offer thee. Those gifts refuse,
That for an instant you delay to choose.
Receive from me the worthiest—her whose charms
Haste to their home in thy adoring arms,
Helen of Argos."

     Then she paused: the word
Ran echoing through my heart, and sweetly stirred,
And loudly, all its pulses; which she knew,
For to herself a cloud the Goddess drew,
And vanished, all victorious. Happy day,
When Paris judged of Goddesses, for they
By that make Troy proud; by that a queen
I claim from golden Venus.

     You have been
From that hour worshiped: and, as I love thee,
So, many Trojan maidens sigh for me;
Him whom they long for, you alone retain:
Nor do kings' daughters only sigh in vain,
But all the Nymphs.

     I care not for them all,
Once filled with hope of thee—on thee I call,
Through sleepless nights, and when my wearied
   eyes
Close in soft slumbers, in my dreams you rise.
Oh! if unseen you charm me, how would you
Charm me, if by your side? Though far the view,

I burn with flames of worship. Why delay
To follow hope that led the joyful way
To where you are? The voice that called to me,
Hushed all the winds, and calmed the stormy sea.

My sturdy axemen felled the Phrygian pine,
And every tree that loves the tumbling brine,
From rugged Gargarus, crowned with woods, to where
Long Ida lifts her leafy head in air.
Then rose the stately ships; through all their length,
The mighty keel, rib-fastened, laughed in strength,
But shapeless seemed and sluggish, till at last,
Flew the white canvas from the springing mast.
Bright legends deck each pictured stern, the tales
Of Gods grown loving—she, who fanned the sails
That bore me here, not absent, nor was he
Forgot, who shoots Love's darts.

      Then to the sea
We turned the prows, Greece-pointed; but my sire
With mournful words bewailed my rash desire,
And prayed, but vainly prayed, delay. Then came
Cassandra, weird, loose-haired, who cried: "A flame

You bear with you—oh! whither do you go,
Thus ruin-charged? Ah! reckless; and you know
Naught of the baleful fires this journey brings!"
I find the fires—'tis truth Cassandra sings—
But they are Love's own flames. The favoring wind
Has fanned the blaze, but Fear has dropt behind.
Thy shores receive me, fairest Nymph; thy lord
Has bid me sit, and nobly, at his board.
This flows from Fate; I know the heavenly sign,
And Jove decrees that Helen's heart is mine.

Here have I seen the heaped-up wealth of Greece,
The spoils of war, the rich results of peace,
But idly passed them by. My eager view
At first, and now, desires, and only, You.
Wondering, I gazed at first—my wonder grows,
My soul's rapt ardor pause, nor languor knows.
Such thrills, such joyful shocks, my senses stirred,
When Venus smiled on my approving word
At the great trial—but had you been there,
Not Love's great mother had been owned so fair.
For everywhere of thee the rumor blows:
Thee far-off Atlas, thee the Tigris, knows:

No Trojan dame thy rival—nor can fame
E'er speak of beauty but through Helen's name.
But though she fill the earth with praise, 'tis less
Than Helen's self.  Let him despair success,
Who hopes to sing thy just renown—the song
Faints with the burden that it bears along.


What wonder, then, the Grecian king admired—
From myriad beauties, only thee desired;
Sought thee in rapine rude, while in the game
Your veilless beauty glowed, nor dreamed of shame?
I praise the theft—but how, oh! how restore
The matchless charms which in his arms he bore!
I should for ever hold such dear delight,
Nor yield thee up to Gods, nor Death's dread might;
My arms should ever clasp; and fed with bliss,
Immortal were the look, the sigh, the kiss.
Should Fate demand, my heaven-defying pride
Would cling to thee, though yielding all beside.
I scorned the World's command, to gain your love,
The royal bounty of the spouse of Jove;

I scorned the wisdom that Minerva gave—
Enough of wisdom this, to be your slave.
Nor does the choice repent me—oft as you
Rise to my fancy, I the choice renew;
Renew each rapturous dream, and vow to gain
Her for whose sake 'twere light to bear all pain.

Nor fear, O nobly born! your queenly state
Will aught diminish, if you share my fate.
Whoever questions of the Trojan line,
Shall find the stars of heaven, and Jove divine.
The sceptred Priam, o'er the boundless plains
Of fertile Asia, proudly, safely, reigns;
Lord of innumerous cities, marches fair,
And temples worthy of the name they bear;
But mightiest, Troy, whose turrets, pointing high,
Rose, 'mid immortal music, to the sky;
Whose pouring crowds surpass the sum of men,
Till scarce can earth the mighty host sustain.
Thee with warm welcomes, and with flying feet,
Shall all the Trojan maids and mothers meet;
Oft, when you think of Greece, will you compare
With Trojan wealth Achaia's petty share.

—But cease, my boastful heart, nor dare despise
The land that gave a Helen to my eyes;
But still unworthy, for a richer earth
Than ours would scarce deserve to give her birth.
Oh! give this beauty every sweet delight,
And taste the sacred joys it claims, of right;
Fill pleasure's goblet up, nor scorn to share
With me, because a Phrygian name I bear;
For he, the foremost of the Phrygian kings,
To Jove in heaven, immortal nectar brings;
Another was Aurora's spouse; and he
Was Phrygian too, whom Venus came to see,
And staid to love, in Ida.

And I dare,
Myself with Sparta's king, thy spouse, compare,
In courage, age, desert. The peaceful night
Shall not be robbed from thee by dread affright
Of thine own husband's sire, before whose eyes,
In glooms of dusk, his horrent victims rise.
Pure is our lineage from the bloody stain
That dyed the waves of all the Grecian main.

—But shall these dreadful themes disturb your
    breast?
All these are nothing—only make me blest.
I hope—but ah! how hopeless: in your arms
Another tastes the sweets of Helen's charms;
And sharing joys for which the Gods might sigh,
Leaves me, in envious pain to faint and die.

Let me recall my griefs: each evening's feast
Finds me an eager but an anxious guest;
And such my jealous pangs, no greater woe
Could I desire for my severest foe;
Such I endure, when, rude as Scythian bear,
Thy husband trifles with thy golden hair,
Toys with thy fingers, and, distasteful theme,
Scarce, in my presence, leaves me aught to dream.
Surely, thy duty, not love's rapture true,
Compels endurance, and an answer too.
—But let me shun the all-abhorrent view,
And when thy drunken lord imprints a kiss,
Hide from my eyes the sight of wasted bliss,
Though from my heart my choking feelings rise,
And all my aching soul dissolves in sighs;

Yet, wanton! with my griefs your laughter grows,
And in my torture, still you find repose.

Nor wine allays the rage of my desire,
The generous draught but adds a flame to fire;
Lest I should see or hear, I turn away,
But when you look or speak, I must obey.
Oh! say what I shall do: to see, is pain;
A greater sorrow 'tis to gaze in vain.
Ah! if I could my love conceal or kill,
Then blest contentment all my heart should fill.
But vain to hope such ending; still appears
My yearning love, and still I toss with fears.
Shall I keep silence, still you know my grief,
And know that you alone can bring relief.
How oft, to hide my tears, a feigned excuse
Brings a short absence from thy lord's abuse;
How oft I feign of ancient love a tale,
To hide my own, and yet my own reveal;
Praise some fond, unknown lover—and so well,
That only you discern what I would tell.

Once, I remember, when the feast was high,
Your beauty doubly glowed on every eye.

Though jeweled robes your perfect form obscured,
Still, through the cloud not less the star allured.
Through wavy seas of dress appeared thy form,
And took my beating, raptured heart by storm.
So was I tranced, the golden cup I bore
Fell from my hand, and rolled along the floor.
You kissed your daughter then—those kisses I
Snatched from her lips before their soul could fly;
Then sang again such songs as you might ask,
And o'er my features drew a cautious mask ;
For such you bid me wear, that none may know
The cause of Helen's pride and Paris' woe.

Despairing all, and chafing at my fate,
I bribed the smiling nymphs who round you wait,
Who gave me naught of hope, but greater fears,
And checked my prayers, and wondered at my tears.
They know not Jove's decrees, nor dream the fate
That waits thee, flying to a mightier state.
Thee shall the victor win by toilsome days,
For thee shall armies fight and cities blaze;
Thy lot shall shame those legends all have read,
Of how for love the great Alcides bled.

Greater than these shall be your deathless name,
Prize of my labors, mistress of my fame.
Than me the prize is more—my humbler share
Is but to woo thee with a lover's prayer.
O Honor, Glory, Brightest Star of Love,
Divinest daughter of immortal Jove!
Hence will I bear thee to the Trojan shore,
Or, here an exile, see my home no more.

No common wound deprives my soul of rest,
And keen the arrow that has pierced my breast.
True was her dream, who saw from out the sky
The Archer launch his shaft, and saw me die.
But you can save me—you and only you;
Love's mother promised this, and she is true.
To you she lends a ready ear to-day—
Ah! fear to drive her kindly aid away.

Too long I linger—words have lost their power;
Now, now the fates attend, 'tis Love's own hour.
Oh! fear not him whom fate has made your spouse,
A careless lord, nor mindful of his vows.
Ah! simple Helen, charming, rustic maid,
Think you that beauty loves such lawful shade?

Oh! be not beautiful—or let your charms
Receive their tribute in a lover's arms.
No other choice is thine. In maid or wife,
Reserve and Beauty wage an endless strife.
How oft the softer conquers, let the sky
Home of the gods and happy souls reply.
Nor does your lineage bid me hope in vain,
If Leda's fire but live in you again.
—Let others vainly hope—if o'er the sea
You fly with Paris, leave their fate to me.

My prayers thy husband seconds, grants his aid;
Time, place, and absence, all things smooth have
    made.
The Cretan realm demands his instant care,
And his safe wisdom has no fears to spare—
Oh! wondrous wisdom! "Helen, I commend,
While absent, to thy dearest care, my friend:
Spare naught to make him happy." Is it so,
Ungrateful one, from whom my torments flow?
Me you defraud, whose quick responsive soul
Draws life from thine, and yields to thy control.
—But should you give that heartless man a heart,
To wake Love's fires there, would pass thy art.

No, if he prized thy heart—thy arms—thy smiles—
He would not leave thee thus to others' wiles.
'Tis he who tempts—not I: and weak my voice,
When his ingratitude suggests the choice.
When he compels, can you advise delay,
Or suffer time, unblest, to slip away?
'Tis he who brings the lover, pleads his cause;
'Tis he who bids you love—obey his laws,
Nor scorn the wisdom of thy spouse discreet,
Who flies—and leaves a lover at your feet!

Alone at night I watch the wheeling Bear;
To Jove your chamber sends a lonely prayer.
Oh! join the prayer, the vigil: let the joy
Of hearts united, day and night employ.
Then I will swear by what you wish; the shrine
Of our dear vows shall be your heart and mine:
Then I, a present lover, all shall dare,
And you shall hear and sigh, and grant my prayer,
Consent to flight, nor once of danger dream,
While yet my lips keep up the ardent theme.

But if you fear, let not examples fail,
And such as might o'er Dian's self prevail.
Ægides, first, and next thy brothers twain,
Wooed thus their brides, nor was the wooing vain.
Than these, no instance nearer to thine eyes,
For me reserved the fourth, most beauteous prize.
Now wait my men, now swell the Trojan sails,
Short be our path before the prospering gales;
Through the rich cities of the Asian plain,
Thyself, a queen, full honors shall obtain.
Thee shall the wondering crowd a Goddess call,
Before thy steps shall fairest matrons fall;
Flames, incense-bearing, shall illume thy road,
And kings shall kiss the spot thy feet have trod.

Alas! for me, who only tell a part
Of what shall happen; thy all-conquering heart
Shall hasten more events than Trojan love,
And fast the Fates upon thy path shall move.
But fear thou not, lest cruel wars pursue—
Lest Greece should swear revenge, and prove too
    true.
What dame of all the dames that e'er have fled,
Has war pursued, or who for such has bled?

Review the names, the histories of the fair,
And doubt if you can doubt their lot to share!
'Tis true, they feared at first; but fear was all—
No danger followed, nor did death appall.
And she who dreaded once lest earth should rise,
Now fears no storm outside her lover's eyes.

But grant the worst—if war assail our path,
Let them beware who rouse the archers' wrath.
My men are bold, my weapons true; the land
That bore me, scorns to fear a foe's command.
Strong may thy husband be, but not to one
Is strength confined. No combat will I shun,
Or now, or ever, with his arms; for I,
Scarce from my cradle stept, feared not to die.
In every contest of the youth I vied,
And countless triumphs fed my martial pride,
Nor think that I, whom all the youth attend,
Could not alone thy sacred cause defend.
Point but the man, the mark; my lusty bow
Shall bring the boast of Grecian armies low.
Is such thy husband's arm—is such his glance—
Is he such warrior, wields he thus his lance?

But grant him this, and then I dare deride:
I fight with mighty Hector at my side.
He worth innumerous soldiers: pride of war:
Amid the bloody ranks a blazing star.

And you are worth the contest; let the blare
Of angry trumpets fill the reddening air;
Let battle's tempests rise; if risen for thee,
What pains shall gauge the price of victory?
Should all the earth contend for thee, thy name
Shall live illustrious in eternal fame.
Faint not with timid fear; the Gods obey,
Who prosperous smiling, call thee hence away.
Pledge me thy faith, and fill the measure up
With thy dear hand, of joy, and life, and hope.

## HELENA AD PARIDEM.

Since I thy vows profane have rashly read,
   Pride prompts to answer, virtue not denies.
You, whom we nobly have received, have said
   The words that ne'er should reach a matron's eyes.
Was it for this the favoring winds arose,
   And sped your vessel to the Grecian shore,
That though from land of strangers and of foes,
   We wrote a welcome on our palace door?
Was it for this, you words of insult bore?

How have you come—as enemy or friend?
   Perhaps when this, my just complaint, you read,
Ah! rustic, you will say, who needs defend
   Her life, so chastely pure in thought and deed!
But if I do not sigh with love-sad grace,
   And if I do not gloom with knitted brow,
Still is my fame as scarless as my face;
   And no such man as thou has cause to show,
How I am less unsoiled than mountain snow.

So more I wonder that in me you find,
  Or think you find, a plea for such desire.
Snatched once from home, you fancy that my mind
  Dwells fondly on the theme of lawless fire:
It makes the crime, if one but yield the will,
  But crimeless I, who all unwilling proved;
Nor further fruit had he of all his skill,
  Whose arts heroic showed how well he loved,
Than to convey me back, unhurt, unmoved.

For though his wanton ardor reft the kiss
  I never gave, it gained him naught beside.
But shameless Trojan, not content with this,
  How worse than his your all-demanding pride!
For Theseus spared to urge, when once the flame
  Of maiden honor flashed across his sight;
But glows your heart with no ingenuous shame,
  Nor will you cease to call me from the height
To that wild sea whose shores are tears and night.

Call me not angry, for our sex is kind
  To lovers' madness—but we need be wise,
And she that's lured by Love's pretense, is blind;
  I doubt your love, but not your praise; my eyes

Tell me that I am fair: I need not you
    To tell me this. But women oft have erred
By flattery such as yours, and not more true;
    I might have wronged, to judge ere I had heard—
Now I convict you, by your every word.

But others sin, and matron fame is rare:
    —Is this a cause that Helen's fame should die?
And from my mother's error, do you dare
    To urge my feet from paths of chastity?
Ah! hapless mother; Nature then withdrew
    Her kindly aid when royal lover came,
Her powers assist the god who stoops to sue;
    And if in form of swan he hides his flame,
The maid, deceived and captured, who shall blame?

But should I wander, 'tis in clearest light,
    Nor aught of ignorance should shade the deed;
My mother sank before Jove's wily might:
    But could my fault a godlike tempter plead?

Though well you boast of noble name and race,
    The race from which I came is more sublime:
The blood of kings in long-forgotten days,
    Pelops and Tyndarus, in later time,
    And then great Jove and Leda's hallowed crime.

For you, 'twere better that convenient shade
    Should drape the foundings of your boasted state;
If ere Laomedon the record fade,
    Naught will be missed of all you would relate;
And though thy Troy be strong and rich and wide,
    Not less a crown does rugged Sparta wear;
While you in wealth barbaric rest your pride,
    We boast of men who well the state can bear,
    Can suffer patiently, and nobly dare.

But crowning arguments, the gifts you bring,
    And which you think a goddess well might snare;
And ah! how sweetly you their praises sing:
    But should I e'er your guilty hazards share,
'Twere you should conquer; gifts are naught beside
    The faint and dull expression of the man;
And I would either in clear fame abide,
    Or follow thee, as only woman can,
    Shorn of thy riches; sport of fortune's ban.

Yet gifts are grateful, which the givers make
   Most precious by their giving: we adore
The love they show, not them. The gift may take
   Love's fragrance, and it cannot well be more.
That me you love is all: that loving me,
   You scorned the perils of Cassandra's dream,
And dared the boundless and the angry sea;
   Compared to this, what gifts could I esteem?
   Or how, preferring those, should I a woman seem?


But rashly why recall the festal hour,
   Whose blushing memories I would fain conceal?
Ah! ardent eyes, whose practised, fatal power
   Implants those wounds their lord alone can heal.
Then would you sometimes sigh, and when the health
   Went round, you drank in cups my lips had kissed;
And oft your fingers spoke in silent stealth;
   And oft your eye-lids, eloquent in mist
   Of sacred tears, your love might well assist.

And then, for fear my lord should all perceive,
   I paled the blush, that redly strove to rise,
But softly spoke unheard, " To grant him leave
   The least, would bring such storm as never dies,
For he would stop at nothing." I was right,
   But yet with playful finger wrote in wine,
That on the table lay within your sight,
   A sparkling AMO; yet the fault was thine,
If you in earnest read such trifling sign.

But, ah! alas! for me, that I should teach,
   My all too cunning tempter what to say;
He who would lead my steps to err, would reach
   My foolish heart in some such flattering way:
Thine is the charm of manhood's beauty too,
   No maiden's heart toward thee could coldly beat:
Choose then the fairest—innocently woo:
   I will resign thee, and with chaste deceit
Your praises calmly to your bride repeat.

Learn then from me, who curbs desire is wise,
   And learn how great the virtue to abstain;
And do you think that you alone have eyes?
   Have others not desired what you would gain?

You see no clearer, but you bolder dare;
    Nor have you more of heart, but less of shame.
Why came you not on wings of eastern air
    When all the kings for me, a maiden, came?
    I would have chosen thee, then, nor dreamed of blame.

This will my husband pardon, when I say,
    Had I seen thee, I ne'er had chosen him;
But now you tardy come to take away
    His joys, long dowered, and your hope is dim;
And what you seek, another holds; but I,
    Who here am chained to Menelaus' side,
Let me conceal from thee how oft I sigh
    That I am not in Troy, thy blameless bride,
    Where in deep peace I might with thee abide.

Cease then, I pray, to rend this tender breast,
    Nor harm me, helpless, whom you say you love;
Oh! let my state, as fixed by Fortune, rest,
    Nor thou a harsh and shameless victor prove.

But Venus promised me; in Ida's vales
  Three shining stars of heaven before thee glowed,
But Juno's power, or Pallas' wisdom, pales
  Before her glittering wiles, who Helen showed
  And taught of conquering love the easy road.

Shall I believe that thus celestials deign
  Confess a mortal than themselves more wise?
But grant it true: the rest you surely feign,
  That I was promised as the fairest prize.
My charms are less than this, that in the mind
  Of goddess I should be of gifts the best;
Content be she who well hath pleased her kind;
  I leave to Venus' self to please the rest,
  Nor let her, false as fair, my peace molest.

But, no; I claim a woman's right to change:
  I trust your story, I accept the praise,
Nor wonder thou, my former doubt so strange:
  Faith slowly grows—a plant of many days—
In all events of moment: but when grown,
  It lives securely. I delight to please
The laughter-loving Venus, and I own
  That I commend whome'er in Helen sees
  Rewards that mock the gifts of goddesses.

And am I wisdom more than Pallas bore,
    A royal kingdom more than Juno held
With outstretched arm, when tempting? I were more
    Than mortal, obdurate, if then I steeled
My breast against your love. Not iron I—
    No stubborn gale am I, from winter land;
But can I love, with whom I cannot fly?
    Of what avail, to plough the salt sea's strand,
Or nurse a hope against the Fates' command?

Nor versed am I in Love's sweet wiles: the art—
    Be Gods my witnesses—to thus betray
My lord, I ne'er have learned: a novel part
    Is this, which now, with silent pen, I play.
Oh! happy they more skilled; for innocence
    Will ever find in guilt a thorny road;
Hedged in with spectres that confound the sense.
    In every eye some evil I forbode,
And rumor follows fast with growing load.

The whispers of the curious crowd I hear;
    My very servants babble to the air;
But you dissemble—he can jest at fear
    To whom my fall immortal fame would bear.

Oh! spare my name—for left behind my lord,
  Whom fateful causes call so far away,
I mourn so slight was my dissuading word,
  When at the vessel's side I cried: "Oh! stay,
  Or let return be balked by no delay."
He joyful kissed me. "Dearest, I commend
  To you the state, the home, the Trojan guest."
I hid a smile, but quick replied: "I lend
  A ready ear, my lord, to your request."
Now on the Cretan sea he spreads his sails,
  But therefore not too rashly shall you dare;
Though he be absent, still his watch prevails;
  To him his trusty spies our actions bear,
  THE ARMS ARE LONG THAT KINGS ARE WONT TO WEAR.

He hath been warned betimes—he justly fears.
  Such praise as thine would warn a duller soul;
And should my beauty lead to shame and tears,
  He would aver that he had known the whole.
But still he trusts. In danger, left behind,
  Not blindness—not neglect—has left me here:
My fame, my life, convince that he shall find
  His Helen's honor, as her beauty, clear—
  And shall I trifle with this heart sincere?

But, ah! my love is stronger than my will,
　And holds the gates of my divided breast.
Why is my lord away—why night so still?
　And why beneath this roof does Paris rest?
Why does thy pleading form possess my mind,
　As bright and fair as ever woman won?
All things invite, compel me to be kind.
　What fear delays that I should be undone,
　Or why so tardy you—and I alone?

'Tis yours to drive away my rustic fear,
　With loving violence to storm my heart;
Thus making happy whom you hold most dear,
　And gaining all, by conquering but a part.
Else must you quench and kill the new-born fire:
　A little water quenches recent flame—
Nor couple thanks of guest with such desire,
　As, fraught with tragic woe, with Jason came
　To fair Hypsipyle, of mournful fame.

Where is Ænone—whom you loved so long,
　And left to languish in th' Idean vale?
Ah! faithless lover: I should do you wrong,
　Could I not tell of all your life the tale.

It says that constant you can never be,
   Though much you vow. But now the winds arise,
And now your comrades call you to the sea :
   Leave, then, the joys that mock your eager eyes,
   Nor think to capture me with worn-out sighs.

I wish it not, that through the listening land
   Swift-flying Fame should tell of my disgrace :
Before the mocking world shall Helen stand,
   Proclaimed as false in heart as fair in face ?
What would thy father, what thy mother, say—
   And all the Trojans? Could you hope me true ?
You who persuade my faltering feet to stray—
   Shall I be ever faithful liege—but you
   Retain the open path—the lawless view !

Whatever stranger walks the streets of Troy,
   Would be to thee a source of anxious dread,
And oft would you the captious threat employ,
   Lest I but follow where you oft have led ;
At once the author and the judge of crime.
   —Let me escape the sentence and the snare,
The boasted riches of your Trojan clime,
   The golden presents that your matrons bear,
   To deck the shame that they would fear to share !

Oh! spare me, wealth-fatigued. Of small esteem
    Are power, riches—me they cannot move;
But home-sick, weary, by Scamander's stream,
    Oh! who would bring to me a heart-sprung love?
Full old—full oft-repeated—are the tales
    Of woman lured to lay her virtue by;
—Behold yon barks that drive with shattered sails;
    By zephyrs fanned, beneath a peaceful sky,
They left the port—for shipwreck! And shall I?


All nature warns me. In the burning brand
    Thy mother dreamed she bore, in bearing thee,
I read the fateful, ominous command,
    That I a Trojan's lawless fire should flee.
I fear Cassandra's dream. And more I fear,
    Because the goddess whom you judged the prize,
Has brought the dreadful hate of Juno here.
    Now blood-stained spears are crossed before my eyes,
And hostile swords against our love arise.

Oh! can you dream my lord will tamely bear,
  Or that his brother will consent to shame?
Though well you boast, and martial aspect wear,
  From Mars' grim spoils has never sprung thy fame.
Let heroes war : do you but only love.
  Let Hector fight for us; whom most we praise.
In other combats, you will worthier prove—
  Dear strife of love, in which victorious bays
  Are won without the loss of peaceful days.


Now should I tell you of the place and hour
  Where they might meet who burn with love's own fire,
Then should I trust too much to lawless power:
  Far off are you from what you most desire!
Yet not, too hasty, chide a safe delay :
  This letter, conscious of my roving mind,
Assists to flight. To-night my maids will say
  To you, "To-morrow, Helen will be kind,"
  And trust me—I'll not say that they are blind!

## LOVE'S FINDING.

There came a voice to me,
One Summer's day, that said: Go forth, and see
The Daughters of the Earth, for they are fair,
And she who, yet unknown, thy lot shall share,
Unknowing, looks for thee.
The Earth is full of beauty everywhere—
The hills, the clouds, the streams,
All blend within thy happy dreams;
Till now, they satisfy thy soul,
Till now, they seem of life the whole,
And thou hast said, What more do I require?
Lo, from this hour, I wake a new desire!

Yet, had I played
Among the flowers with many a little maid,
Our merriment and fun
Commencing with the sun,
Ceased not, till evening brought unwilling sleep.
Had I the boyish record failed to keep

Of stolen kisses—stolen, when I might
As well have snatched them in the noonday light,
Or published them to all—so meaningless,
So harmless, jocund, void of all excess,
Free of all consequence,
The very heart of youthful innocence.

But why
The altered look, demeanor wistful, shy,
Of those who lately romped upon the lawn,
And tossed the ball, and chased the birds at dawn,
With me: what veil was thrown,
So strangely sudden, o'er what I had known,
Obscuring, changing every feature?
And I, too, had become another creature,
And nursed a pride that came, I knew not whence,
And seemed a new, another sense.
I seemed to fear
Lest any one should come too near,
And spy defect in what was not yet grown;
Safer to be alone,
Safer to nurse unseen the kindling spark
Of what, I knew not; hidden yet in dark,

Concealed as well from me, but still possessed
I knew, because it gave no rest,
But ever burned, uneasy, in my breast.

As in a cloud I moved,
Beyond whose folding mists the voice beloved
Was heard, that called me on
To shining realms of sun,
Unseen, but heralded by shafts of light,
Making all the heavens bright.

Ah! sweet uncertainty—the trembling air,
Whose waves the harp's vibrations bear,
Moves not more blissfully,
Nor more unconsciously,
Of its sweet burden, than my soul's desire,
Which swayed me hither, thither, ever nigher
The unknown place where I would be,
The glimmering shore of mystic sea,
On which the waves of love sighed tranquilly.

And then she came,
Who gave my thought a name;
No matter how, or when, or where,
Her presence answered my soul's prayer;

Whether in moonlight beams arrayed,
First dawned upon my sight the maid,
On hill, by fountain, or in grove,
Or on some careless summer rove,
Up the green valleys where the gleam,
O fair Connecticut! of thy abundant stream,
Makes all the landscape glad ; or haply met
On giant mountain, firmly set
Deep in the humble earth, whose lordly peak
Climbs skyward—but can aught more sadly speak
The barrenness of solitude ?
Such of New Hampshire's Kings, the mood.
Or whether met in scene of mirth,
Keeping time with joyous bound,
While the happy earth
Underneath the midnight stars went round ;
Or in a garden, where the lily and rose,
All summer swaying to each breeze that blows,
Show her sweet skill, who thus prolongs
The time of flowers, birds, and songs.

But where she lingered, there
I hastened my allegiance to declare ;

But sudden, paused: with quick and sharp distress,
There rose in me the sense of deep unworthiness,
To be to her what I would be;
Nor could I to myself confess
That I was what she wished to see.
Such hold hath undeserving pride!
It seemed that by some happy tide,
The better part of life had floated to my side;
Yet what I had been, shrank from laying claim
To that bright form, whose stainless fame
Put all myself, and all my life, to shame.

Then, while dismay
Held o'er my conscious soul such troubled sway,
More fair she seemed, and still more fair,
As more despairing grew Despair.
The world had hailed her beautiful: to me
Appeared what others did not see:
Within her face all my life's hope,
Of all my powers and thoughts the scope;
The measure of my dreams; the goal
Whither, heavenward, ran my soul.
In her eyes' kindliness,
Other saw friendliness;

But I, ineffable society,
Promise of joy without satiety,
Sympathy without a bound,
And tenderness with passion crowned;
Though not yet mine,
No other monarch should she ever own:
Should not our lives combine,
Each were eternally alone.

Then to myself my mocking heart did say,
Fly swiftly, and forever, far away
From her who humbles thus thy worth.
What, is she not of human birth,
And fed and reared as thou?
To man should woman bow,
As he will see who will but look
Abroad on Nature's ample book:
Upward, downward, everywhere—
Man is no exception there.
Use brief empire as she will,
Woman is the lesser, still;
And if thy dream lead thee astray,
Humbly woman to obey,

Better to wake: though for a season,
Waking to thy manhood's reason
Fill thee with sorrows and with pain,
Soon will strength return again.
Happy he who thus is freed
From humbling and tormenting need.

There came a better moment, when
I answered to this voice again.
Nature's true promptings these, that stir
All my soul to worship her.
Her volume, everywhere outspread,
Says now what it hath always said—
Worship goodness, truth, and beauty,
Pride should follow after duty.
Though lesser sinewed, Woman is my mate—
Or more, in all that makes humanity's estate.
Sweet prompter of noble deeds, she ever has brought
The better complement of human thought.
That one sweet soul most humbly I adore,
Makes me not less than man, but more.
So will I love and worship, nor shall shame
Falsely speak to me of blame.

Then clear my pathway seemed, and I
Hastened to her side to fly,
And tell her all, with word sincere,
Such as she could not choose but hear,
Even if hearing barred consent.
Thus my passion outward went
To her; boundless waves of feeling,
All myself concealing
In their mighty flow—
Such as, if maiden do but know,
Or understand in thousandth part,
Force the gateway of her heart;
If, of a thousand passionate words thus spoken,
One but welcome enter
To the guarded centre
Of her heart, then every guard is broken!

—Was this a dream, that she did condescend
Her being with my own to blend,
And make me master of her soul,
Till now by maidenly control
Safe tutored, hid from every eye,
And most of all, when I was by?

## LOVE'S FINDING.

Oh! sweetest joy that lover meets,
The vanishing of love's deceits;
Of veils the maiden subtly wears,
When, ere accepted, he appears
Half foe, half friend: they say, Beware,
Much must thou overcome to enter here;
The task is great, but great beyond compare
The prize, if Beauty take thee to her sphere!
Doubly, trebly, is he thwarted—
She smiles on others, strangely looks on him:
Often has he started,
Fearing lest he be the sport of mocking whim,
Till some sign assures him; then again,
Cared for least he seems of all the world,
A moment raised by fancy vain,
Then back to darkness hurled.
Such moods hath love accepted, banished.
Veil and subtlety have vanished:
Kindly, under love's clear sun,
Maiden owns that she is won.


O vision sweet!
How often do my thoughts repeat

What thought can never reach, or word express,
That untold loveliness
Reflected on the heart that sees
In other heart its happy destinies!
Does she, who thus is mirrored, know
How her reflected graces glow
Upon the soul of him who sees in her
The mystic charms that all his being stir?
Then would she ever soar above
The frailties, weaknesses, that others move,
And live in that celestial air,
Whither ascends of passionate love the prayer;
Alas! mistaking or despising Love,
How oft are possible seraphs kept from rising there!

Thus much written, when I came
To where she sat, for praise or blame,
Whatever might my lines deserve; but she
Heard them through, then said to me,
All is nothing that you write.
Pen, though fed by morning light,
May glorify a maid or man,
But picture love it never can.

Needs it no apology,
No praise we need to love it by;
And those who know it, know it well, without
Those passionate tints that make the careless doubt,
Whom you will never teach. Hope thou before,
That moles will to the upper heaven soar!

## TEDIUM VITÆ.

### I.

To-night I hear the sad familiar strain
    That all the sorrowing ages join to sing;
Though wine and mirth may banish it, again
    It creeps upon us, forced to listening.

### II.

Such strains our happy childhood never heard,
    Attuned to chords whose only breath was joy;
Or if by ruder, harsher impulse stirred,
    The sorrow was but wonder to the boy.

### III.

The hour delayed, must come. Reluctant doubt,
    If Pleasure's form be not her ghost instead,
Must yield to certainty; henceforth, without
    The dear illusion, sadly must proceed

IV.

Our shortening days; and never more returns
    The bloom, the fragrance, or the flush of life;
And if Ambition's fire still ardent burns,
    Ah! what avails the fierce and dusty strife

V.

Through which it lights our pathway? What is fame,
    Or honor, flattery, wealth, estate, or praise,
To blissful hours, when, innocent of blame,
    Kind o'er us smiled the wondrous, long-drawn days?

VI.

Each day a blessed mystery. The sun,
    Fresh sprung, made consecrate the golden East,
And long before his westering course was run,
    The lingering day had been an endless feast.

VII.

Deep hid in meadow-grass we conned the sky;
    The boblink warbled o'er us as we lay;
And, murmuring pleasant bass, the brook ran by,
    And o'er the pebbles sang its life away.

### VIII.

How overflowed with happiness the hours,
    When free of thought, as waves that lap the shore,
We sought in woodland glens the dewy flowers,
    Or home a wealth of ripened blueberries bore.

### IX.

Or wrapped in pleasant fancies, which we knew
    In naught, except without them, lonesome we;
We crowned the little maids with fealty due,
    And hailed them queens, beneath the chestnut tree.

### X.

All friends were kind, all love was true, and most
    The love that stirred and woke one happy day,
And bore us to a warm and fragrant coast,
    On strong, swift wings, that knew not of delay.

### XI.

And there we found the crowning joy; to this
    Was all life shaped, and this the perfect end;
And Life and Love united in the kiss,
    Where all long-past, forerunning joys did blend

### XII.

And there should life have ended. What, the rest,
    But once exhausted joy—increasing pain?
If from the banquet-board we take the best,
    Why try the waning, narrowing choice again?

### XIII.

From every height, the path must downward go;
    Nor firm abiding there, will Fate permit.
Oh! bravely linger, if descent be slow,
    We less perceive, we readier yield to it.

### XIV.

Yet linger vainly. Years with swift increase,
    Inexorably bear us down, to where
The highest joy that man can ask, is peace,
    And pains are light that end not in despair.

### XV.

We lose the sun's bright rays as we descend—
    If still he shine, he shines to other eyes;
And more our melancholy glances tend,
    Where ominously hang the western skies.

### XVI.

The warm, electric thrill of twenty-one,
   That made the friend the sharer of the heart,
Has long departed; we have colder grown,
   And rest our faith in wisdom's shrewder art.

### XVII.

And saddest change of all, the gentle maid,
   Whose impulse once was sweetest charity,
Whose whispers underneath the summer shade,
   Sincerely breathed of Love and Peace, to me—

### XVIII.

Ah! why should haggard memory recall
   The dream? Unworthy husband, blasting years,
Too surely conquer. If a seraph fall,
   The mournful ruin who shall gauge with tears?

### XIX.

The senses fail. Where now the vision keen,
   That tracked the eagle through the sun-lit sky,
And left no beauties of the world unseen?
   Uncertain shadows now, they pass us by.

### XX.

Or when the goblets flash around the board,
  And wit and song prolong the festal night,
Can rarest wine, from crystal beakers poured,
  Awake the flush of youthful appetite?

### XXI.

And verses weary, music dully falls;
  The ear, grown critical, too early tires;
No rhythmic harmony, but soon it palls
  On him who feebly, languidly admires.

### XXII.

And selfish grown, we widely sit apart,
  And nurse our silent and our separate schemes.
Our lips no more convey from heart to heart
  The frank recital of ingenuous dreams.

## TO A DAY IN MARCH.

### I.

Day not more fair than many days,
Nor ruled by sure or sunny skies,
And less deserving Poets' praise,
When vernal songs arise,
Than those that after come,
Breathing May blossoms out upon the air,
Or scattering June's red roses round our home,
Yet I to sing thy praise will always dare.

### II.

To me a welcome thou shalt bring,
Since envious years must surely roll,
When first the young and timid spring,
Creeps slowly to the pole.
Though birds delay to fly,
Delay their passionate song, delay the nest;
Yet love keeps pace with thee along the sky,
And brings familiar gladness to my breast.

### III.

Speak ever to the faithful hearts
Of two who watch thy coming well,
To whom the day a joy imparts
Beyond this verse to tell;
The self-same words of hope
That once descended softly from the blue,
And from thy mild and fleecy clouded cope,
Fell on our reverent heads like gentlest dew.

## LUCY.

I saw, when late he left the ball,
    Through eyes grown somewhat dim and tired,
That you—'twere best concealed from all—
    That you admired.

Yet, gentle maiden, you confess
    Not even to yourself the thought;
And who am I, that I should press
    Advice not sought?

For though the glances of your eye,
    Treacherous, your feelings quick betrayed,
What right has stranger thus to spy,
    And thus invade

The secrets of your virgin heart?
    But plain to him, who not excels
In love-craft, you can have no part
    Where other dwells

Already.  Spare the fruitless sigh,
   Half-heaved and sudden-checked.  Ah! vain,
If Love uncalled, too early fly,
   He falls again.

Hope not.  For you no resting-place
   Exists, or can, within his breast;
Through all his visions glides a face,
   Obscures the rest:

Than yours no fairer.  You are fair;
   But fairer you than Paphian doves,
Or Vashti, you could not compare
   With her he loves.

Forget—forget in time: for now
   The thought is friendly to your soul,
And fits for future love: but how,
   If past control?

Not weakness, checked.  The common fate
   It is, to suffer.  He who jests
At you, with vultures well might mate—
   And they the best!

Forget—but only him.   Let Love
 Still rule your breast with welcome power,
The heavens will surely bounteous prove,
 Some happier hour.

## THE STREAM AT THE NORTH.

WHERE gray Tahawus lifts his head
   High in the northern air,
And nodding plumes of hemlock boughs,
   Obscure the noonday glare,
A noisy river courses o'er
   A bed of opals rare.

In hidden clefts of mountain caves,
   Its living springs arise,
Known only to the deer who shuns
   The watchful hunter's eyes,
And having quenched his eager thirst,
   Back to his covert flies.

O fair that brook to him who wooes
   The goddess of the wood,
Who seeks to win her loving smiles
   In her own solitude,
And offers grateful sacrifice
   Upon her altars rude.

But fairer is that bright wood-stream
   To him who, loving well
Nature in all her myriad forms
   Of which the poets tell,
Has ever found his feet incline
   To where the Naiads dwell:

And in the swiftly-rushing floods,
   Where spotted troutlets shine,
Eclipsing in their ruddy glow
   The splendors of the mine,
With beating heart and skillful arm
   Has cast the quivering line:

For in these crystal waves he finds
   The sum of all his dreams;
What time, in visions of the night,
   He tried those wondrous streams,
Which, in the angler's Paradise,
   Are white with scaly gleams.

With joyful heart and bounding foot,
   He takes his eager way
To the cool banks, when faintly breaks
   The dawn of morning gray ;
And when across the whirlpool slants
   The sun's declining ray.

Treading by pools whose darkling depths
   Elude the fearful eye,
He scales the wet and oozy crags
   From which the foam-wreaths fly ;
And finds the broad and rapid shoals
   Where trout at evening lie.

Then with his trusty hatchet frames
   A cabin rude of bark ;
And soon his camp-fire's spiral darts
   Shoot up into the dark ;
And o'er the dusky forest boughs
   Whirls many an eddying spark.

And thus by day his pulse is high,
   By night his dreams are sweet;
And when unto the world of men
   Again he turns his feet,
He feels his soul and frame prepared
   Its heavy cares to meet.

Bright stream, unto thy mossy banks
   Long may the red deer go;
Amid the Adirondack wilds,
   Thy opal waters flow;
And to the angler's loving eyes,
   Their fruitful beauties show.

# GALLIA CAPTA.

**WRITTEN IMMEDIATELY AFTER THE COUP D'ETAT.**

### I.

The nation, vexed by more than ancient pains,
  In dull submission wastes the fruitless year;
Her city walls are red with shameful stains,
  And men are dumb with fear.

### II.

Her long-descended standards, late so proud,
  And flaunted gaily out before the world,
Are drooped beneath a black, impervious shroud—
  In dust and darkness furled.

### III.

The name whose mention sent a sudden shock
  Of leaping terror to the farthest lands,
Sublimely potent on the Baltic rock—
  Amid the Libyan sands;

### IV.

Obscures its glories.  He who bears it now,
    At once the shame and strength of all his race,
Has girt a purchased crown about his brow,
    And wears a twofold face:

### V.

A new-born Janus, armed with horrid frown,
    With threats whose consummation follows fast,
With cunning words that keep the people down,
    And cheat them to the last.

### VI.

Submissive turning to the Northern god
    At whose command he plays his coward part,
With smiling face attentive to the nod
    That nerves his fearful heart.

### VII.

The world is waiting.  Justice hides her beam,
    And plants her sword within the sluggish ground;
And human fancies, in divided stream,
    Emit a dubious sound.

### VIII.

Perhaps a passing mist obscures the light
  Of that clear star that on the nations burned;
Perhaps the thick-hung clouds that brought the night,
  Will soon be backward turned.

### IX.

Or gloomier terror may enshroud the land,
  From mightier hands the wrathful vials flow;
Till in the silent dark the people stand,
  Engulfed in hopeless woe.

# EPIGRAMS FROM MARTIAL.

### AD CECILIANUM.

My friend, before you won your wife,
No suitor e'er disturbed her life;
But since—you guard her with such care,
That people think there's something there,
And now she's all the rage. A word with you:
While she is neither seen nor heard—she'll do!

### IN PHILONEM.

Philo, up and down through Rome,
Swears he never dines at home.
"Prodigious fellow!" People say:
"What, asked to dinner every day?"
Not so fast—he's often slighted—
Four times a week, at least, he's not invited,
And then, the sycophantic sinner
Has no chance at all of dinner!

## SOPHIA.

You smiled on me, when first the smile
  Of woman filled my soul with pleasure;
And, all my fancy free of guile,
  I, boyish, eager, grasped the treasure

Thus offered. Then you thronged my dreams
  In every shape of grace and love;
A thousand glances—thousand gleams
  Of new-born sunlight from above.

How stirred my senses then! A new,
  Fresh life had dawned. Then passed away
All former joys, and, following you,
  I lived in Love's perpetual day.

I hymned you in a thousand songs;
  For you I beggared land and sky;
I said: Whate'er to Earth belongs
  Of Beauty, pales when she is nigh.

And still you smiled, and still you praised,
   And fed me with rewards so sweet—
Ah! why forget that I have raised
   The grave-mound o'er their dear deceit,

Deep buried? Yet their mocking shades
   Glide through the chambers of my heart;
One enters as another fades,
   I would—would not—they might depart.

---

'Twas but a fancy—thus you said—
   A sister you might be; no more.
What gave that moment strength, that dead
   I was not carried from your door?

Oh! but that this unfeeling frame
   O'er the chained mind usurps control,
I had consumed in passionate flame;
   But Nature spares us—pitying soul!

What use to argue? You had taken
　Of life the glory and the bloom:
At once, of these and you, forsaken,
　Could aught dispel or gild the gloom?

Remember now, that I reproved you
　In not a word. With gesture sad,
I said: Sophia, I have loved you,
　And I have given you all I had.

Whatever be the cause that led you,
　Thus, reckless, with my heart to play,
I will not ask it. Then I fled you,
　Nor know I where I went that day.

Oblivion hides it. Let the cloud
　Still linger: let such cloud obscure
All deadly sorrows, that the proud,
　When hidden, only can endure.

Remember, now, that I reproved you
    In not a word.  From manhood's power
Is woman safe: else had I loved you
    Tenfold, your life that very hour

Were forfeit.  What, shall you receive
    The garnered tribute of my heart,
And waste it?  But your sex has leave
    To safely play a treacherous part!

I thought you kindly as your name,
    That, softly flowing, charms the air:—
Let him love you who loves the flame
    That leaves the meadow scorched and bare!

I did not die.  An idle tale
    Is this—that blasted love is death.
Why should my ruddy currents fail,
    Because my heart lies numb beneath?

Who dies?  Some sickly soul lies here,
    Who, while he lived, was scarce alive;
At Love's rebuff he died of fear;
    But they who merit life survive.

And not within your hands is placed
    The bolt of death. Creator wise,
Oft is thy creature, man, disgraced,
    But not from wounded love he dies.

Whatever birthright we have shared,
    Or yielded wholly to the Sex,
Still, from this crowning folly spared,
    Our life survives of life the wrecks.

---

Go, Woman, you have had your day;
    I, whom you injured—I forgive:
The worst for you that I can say,
    Is this: Sophia, go, and live.

The hopes of manhood call me on—
    Friends, reputation, wealth, and fame;
And rises bright o'er all, the dawn
    Of Love that now deserves the name.

Nor less I love, because you taught
    Me how to feel a woman's art:
Not yours is every woman's thought,
    Nor false is every woman's heart.

What have you gained?  A victory here—
    A victory there.  The fruit is light:
Of what avail to you the tear
    I haply shed one bitter night?

Will others love you yet?  Behold,
    Aslant your temples—fatal sign—
The crowfoot!  You are growing old;
    And here the Sex is not like wine.

Oh! let the ripening matron dwell
    In reverence.  You are not as she.
The years that blast the thorn, how well
    They deck the bounteous apple-tree!

Live on, the wonder of the maid
    Who presses manly arm at eve;
Ah! gentle sunbeam of my shade,
    Some souls there be that can't deceive.

Live on: from me no further word;
Live on, and vainly hope repose;
Ever with her who thus has erred,
There troops a sullen host of woes.

# A FINANCIAL EXPERIENCE.

In the city of Hartford—the people of which
Are, with scarce an exception, enormously rich;
Possessed of whole counties and States at the West,
And still having cash that they wish to invest;
And they know how to do it, if any can know,
As their notes, stocks, and bonds will abundantly show—
There lives a warm fellow who makes it his trade
To discount good paper as fast as 'tis made.

In fact, he invites it, and hangs out a sign,
Enticing and eloquent—only one line;
I think it good English—quite free from impurities:
"Money always to lend, on the best of securities."
It gives one great trust in this kindest of men,
To note how precaution presides o'er his gain;
I'd leave him my funds as I pass through the town,
Were they not drawn so closely, alarmingly, down.

## A FINANCIAL EXPERIENCE.

This kindest of creatures, with other good qualities,
Possessed, as is natural, certain partialities.
In dates not particular—shorter or longer—
Where paper is lengthy, the profit is stronger.
But this his chief preference—I own to the same:
He always desired a "favorite name;"
He meant it financially—the name that I hank-
Er for lodges with Cupid, and not at the Bank!

My friend, if you covet wealth, comfort, or fame,
Oh! haste to acquire a favorite name;
For what would become of our snug little dinners,
The pleasures and dainties that cheer us poor sinners,
The luxuries of life that pertain to our station,
Should our banker refuse us all accommodation?
A good name is better than riches, you'll find,
While it lasts, Master Plutus, if paid well, is kind.

One name in especial, he vastly admired,
A dresser of leather—but long since retired;
Punctilious and honest, a trifle too free
With his friendly indorsement; and here, as you see,

Was the source of his profit—not being legitimate
Paper of business, the bank was quite shy of it.
So knowing his safety and wealth of estates,
Our friend always took it, and made his own rates.

But T. Wray, the leather man, being a wag,
And not quite half-liking his paper should drag,
And his neighbors be forced to submit to a shave,
Most fiendishly, wickedly, thus did behave:
He went to a neighbor and thus did he say:
"Make the following note to my order—T. Wray.
And start not in horror, though fearful the style
Of the paper in question—'twill yet make you smile."

*Ne lude cum seriis,* says Wisdom; despite her,
The fault is T. Wray's, not the fault of the writer:
This, then, was the document—brief, but how dismal!
Revealing a perfidy truly abysmal:
*Sixty days after death I promise to pay*
*To the order of Mr. Theophilus Wray,*
*For value received of him, five hundred dollars,*
*At my office on Blank street—Simeon Collers.*

An ominous promise for mortal to make,
Who knows not what course his hereafter will take:
But this is but prosing. The note was completed,
And straight to our friend, Mr. S. Collers fleeted:
Began with some talk in a general way—
The state of the weather, the news of the day;
Diverged to finance by an easy transition,
And lugged out the note in a crumpled condition.

Who ever would think to look Death in the face
On the face of a note? 'Tis a singular place!
No wonder the banker, not dreaming the state
Of the matter, imagined the "death" to be "date."
The "d," "a," and "t" were so large in the joints,
The "e" and the "h" shrunk to minimum points:
Percentage was settled—I have heard of a lower,
And the customer bowed in due form to the door.

The note in collection then quietly rested,
And in due course of time was most promptly
    —protested;
The Notary adding his honest conviction,
The matter was quite beyond law's jurisdiction.

"The note is not due," thus he said in the margin,
"The evidence ample, and needs no enlarging;
I protest for mere form, and yourself, sir, to please,
And I fear that your case is quite weak in the knees,
And I'll thank you to send by the bearer, the fees."

The lawyers were puzzled, till one who had dream't o'er
The case rather longer, said: "*Caveat emptor*—
It is clear that no fraud has been done or intended;
If sued, Mr. Wray can with ease be defended.
In fine," quoth the sapient man of the law,
"The do is as perfect as ever I saw;
Search out, first the drawer, and then the drawee,
Make the best terms you can—and, beg pardon, the fee."

But scarce had our friend reached his office next day,
Quite sick of expenses, when entered T. Wray;
The note, less the discount and charges, to pay,
Provided the Banker thereafter would claim,
Only legalized rates on his favorite name.

And thus the indorser, Theophilus, spoke:
We teach you a lesson by means of a joke;
To take, whether greater or lesser distress it is,
No unfair advantage of people's necessities.

What followed? A dinner of course—and the rest,
Champagne and Good Fellowship—both of the best:
But here is the circumstance worthy of note—
The Banker, though never before had he wrote
Any verses for albums, or papers, or fairs,
And rather avoided such pitfalls and snares,
After some little hemming and mild hesitation,
Propounded this moral with great acceptation:

### MORAL.

##### ADDRESSED TO THE UNFORTUNATE BANKING CLASSES.

Avoid all bills, both small and great,
That run beyond the present state,
    For fear a mortuary date
May give you much too long to wait.

For if you gain the upper air,
You may not find your debtor there;
Or if you haply chance to go
Where fancy rates are charged for snow,
You'll find collections hard and slow!

---

### CROSS PURPOSES.

On the Hudson steamer, to the coke-
Feeder, thus a thirsty traveler spoke:
"Where's the bar?" To which in answer, he:
"Just nine miles this side of Albany!"

# ROSALIA.

Rosalia, often you complain,
Your husband's love begins to wane.
In naught does he neglectful prove,
Affection lives in every act;
But where is now the throbbing love
Of which his being once was all compact?
When dawned the nuptial hour,
Trembling, you feared his love.  Imperial power
It seemed; a gorgeous monarch, waited on by
    bands
Of flying, eager, quick desires,
Innumerous as ocean's sands,
And ardent as the roaring woodland fires.
His love informed your own, thrilled through
    your veins,
Shook your awed soul with joys as fierce as pains,
Made life too sweet to bear,
And filled with dazzling light the sphere
Where you reigned royally when he was near.

When dawned the nuptial hour,
Indeed, Rosalia, love's imperial power
Shone from his eyes.  But, tell me where was then
The love that fitly answered his again?
Unborn as yet; for you were satisfied
Simply to be his bride.
This, to your gentle timid soul,
Seemed to be of love the whole.
You were content to be his treasure,
His source of joy, his fount of pleasure;
Him you sought not, but if desired,
How blest were you to be admired;
How blest were you to be to him a joy,
Which you dreamed not before you could impart;
And happy you, thus always to employ
The passive kindness of your virgin heart.

You married.  Then your love awoke,
Unheard, unknown, till then, your being spoke
To you in accents thrilling, strange, and new,
And love's bright arrows pierced you through.

No sacrifice too great for you to make
For his dear sake,
Whose name you bore; with him most willingly
You would have crossed the land and sea.
Why had your eyes so long been closed
To those perfections where you now reposed
Your trust, your life, yourself? What fortune rare
Had made you mistress there?
Among all maidens, why were you his choice,
Whose smiles had made a Queen rejoice?
Each day, each month, saw love's increase;
You dressed, you sang, you danced, your lord to please,
And only him; the world beside
Unheeded passed. Your only pride
Was He: and if He praised, your soul was satisfied.

But did he love you more
Than he had loved before?
Ah! no. The goldfinch in the air
More sweetly sings
Than when, of human tenderness the care,
Within the cage it folds its wings.

When the forest warbler
In your bosom lies,
Dulled are the bright colors
That once so charmed your eyes.
He loved you none the more,
Because a greater love for him you bore,
But rather loved you less,
Because his own unworthiness,
Known so well to him,
Escaped your penetration dim.
Unsagacious, undiscerning, fondly blind,
Love that loses least respect shall bitter ending find.
Man that reasons, loses reason,
Only in his own desire;
She who would keep his love in season,
Must fear to love with equal fire.

Unwelcome truth—as old as human life:
The maid—the bride—is dearer than the wife.
I know that poets say,
Not so: but what says every day?
O Poets! gild the truth, but don't deny
The iron facts that 'neath the gilding lie.

Let life assert itself, within your song,
Wholly and truly, else the world you wrong,
—Rosalia, never more
Shall you behold the love that once he bore.
But blame him not: did he blame you,
Or doubt if you were true,
Because your love for him seemed cold,
When one light word from you were worth a world
    of gold?
When he tossed throughout the weary night;
Lost his courage, trembled with affright,
If you but careless seemed; then did you share
Such wild love and wild despair?
No; you calmly slept and woke,
Smiled upon him when he spoke,
Walked with him beneath the moon,
Playful, said, "What, home so soon!"
Breathed a kind prayer, and peaceful, slept,
While he on restless couch a weary vigil kept.

In love, as life, if wants are few
How easy 'tis to fill them;
Vain and idle wants subdue,
Or, what is better, kill them.

Follow Nature, if you would
Be happy, wise, and free:
Nature would not, if she could,
Except her laws for thee.
Would you win your husband's love?
Ever keep thyself above
Love's level; let him not possess
Wholly thyself; a little less
Will make him long for all.
Call him upward where you are:
When he reach that station fair,
Higher, farther, call.
Oft be to him a maiden strange,
After whom his thoughts shall range;
Lead him through the flowery path,
Where Imagination hath
Her choicest rove, and let his fancy find
In you the sum of every good combined.
Beware satiety; the sweetest, thence,
Too much, too often tasted, blunt the sense.
Often change your mood; but pride
Keep thee ever dignified,
And maiden-modest. Petulance,
Anger, jealousy, pretense,

Keep these distant from your thought:
Much contempt these evil birds have wrought,
But never love; and such defect
Must surely drive away respect.

Let me not transgress the bound
Where home and husband fence thee round:
But trust me—me who would restore
The love whose loss you now deplore.
Win it—keep it, while you may;
All too soon 'twill fade away:
Who shall Nature disobey?
Soon your winsome beauty fades,
Lo, a troop of laughing children now your hearth invades!
Fresh and joyous, think you, as they play,
Each has helped to steal my youth away?
Man, grown older, in his children lives;
They are of his blood:
For them, his toil he cheerful gives,
And makes them heirs of all his good.
In them he sees perpetuate
His name, his fame, his rising state

Of greatness, wealth—whatever he
Most desires confirmed should be.
They, and they only, without pain,
Recall his days of youth again;
In them he sees his early bloom,
When life had never heard of gloom;
In his friends around, he spies
Crow's-feet springing from the eyes,
Failing senses, waning power,
No promise in the coming hour;
The rose has faded from the cheek
That once so redly blushed, if he but chanced
    to speak;
The ardent gust of life has fled,
Its joyous hopes are crushed—are dead;
But lo! he sees around him stand
A rising, happy, mirthful band,
Who make him young again. For thee—
Best, if thou join their company;
Rosalia, 'tis the stratagem
Will give thee power over him.
Let not the thought of age intrude,
As you look round upon your brood.

Be young with them by happy art,
And gain the vantage of his heart;
Though the daughters please him well,
What! shall you lose, without a sigh,
The old, accustomed spell,
That once you won and kept him by?
Fear not the unequal race,
Let not care invade your face,
Let your smiles be morns of May;
Then, as of old, will he obey:
Or, at the worst, you can but share
The empire with your daughters fair.

But dream not ever to displace,
Rosalia, maiden, bride, or wife,
The sad sub-bass
That underrunneth every woman's life;
See the honors that await
Man's advancing state.
But, long since, flattery
Ceased to fall upon your ear,
Nor, as in days gone by,
Do you but need to speak for all to hear;

No matter how disguised,
At last, on you surprised,
Will fall the world's command; with grace
Content thyself to fill the second place;
In thy husband's name
Be content to find thy fame,
And let thy sons and daughters be
Crowns of honor unto thee.
The day has passed, of her who once was fair,
Her husband's, children's, triumphs now to share,
Becomes her state: nor more ambition gives
To her who after Youth and Beauty lives.

## HELEN.

### I.

The brimming tides of Delaware
   Beyond the meadows gleam;
I see the ships they proudly bear:
   I hear the flowing stream.
The panting ox before the plough
   Enjoys the shade, nor dreams of me;
His master's sturdy shoulders bow
   Beneath the apple tree,
In which I sit, in swaying nest,
   And taste the airs of balmy June,
And wait the hour that makes me blest—
   My heart with summer hours in tune.

II.

Last night, while blew the Southern wind,
    I lay beneath the trees,
And gazing at her window-blind,
    I sang such songs as these:
" Awake, my Queen, for now the night
    Has hushed a world that doubts of Love,
And Love the Conqueror sheds his light—
    The conquered world above.
Yet sleep, my Queen, for happy dreams
    Descend to thee from every star,
And dearer now your lover seems,
    Than any waking thought could dare."


III.

Spur on thy coursers, flaming Sun,
    And haste the trysting hour,
For though my life has just begun,
    The bud is quick to flower.

Though sweet the cool of early morn,
  The shining river's seaward flow,
The songs of birds from heaven borne,
  The hum of earth below;
Yet runs my heart beyond them all,
  To fairer nook of garden shade,
Through which I soon shall walk, and call
  The flying, yet expectant maid.

## SONNET.

You talk of Sentiment: but I renounce it;
The lips are echoes of the mocking heart,
And that false subtlety that takes its start
From out the soul's dark chambers—they pronounce it.
Oh! our two natures—they are rank deceivers;
The inward Counsellor, the outward Act—
The gilded Sentiment, the iron Fact—
Befooling all but practised unbelievers.
True wisdom this: Doubt the fair words of men;
Hear promises, advice, with cautious ears;
Being deceived, be not deceived again;
And watch the deep monitions of your fears.
So shall Success, that well-fed imp, abide
Through an obsequious world, attendant at your side.

Swift rushing River of Life, delay, delay—
Thy endless course one happy moment stay;
Here, on this fragrant bank of summer flowers,
Fain would we linger out the day's sweet hours—
Ah! day too sweet—too brief—so swift the sun,
Half-ended seem our joys, when scarce begun!

Still flows the tide—still drifts our helpless bark—
Still round the world for ever creeps the dark;
Still sinks the sun before it: Life and Light
Yield, and must ever yield, to Death and Night.
Each hour but robs us—longer as we live,
Each robs us more, because we've less to give.

Unequal contest, where th' event is sure,
And courage profits, only to endure—
Our fitful strife with Destiny and Time,
—Hopeless indeed, but none the less sublime—
Where every step is backward, and a wall
Of darkness glooms upon the rear of all.

WHAT lesson graves those hoary rocks,
  Set deeply on the shores of Time,
  Whose fangs far-reaching to the prime,
Sway not by elemental shocks—

Strong songs of deep and lustrous mind;
  Clear annals of the world's long life,
  Sharp truths of argumental strife,
True pictures of our human kind?

Not that in sudden gust of force
  Lives the high secret of the spell,
  By which we too may build as well
Eternal records of our course:

But that the might that rears a Tower
  To be by distant ages spied,
  Grows in the arm by labor tried,
And owns no circumstance or hour.

# FRAGMENTS FROM HORACE.

---

### AD LICINIUM.

#### I.

BEWARE, Licinius, the open sea;
  But while you, cautious, shun its stormy roar,
Avoid with equal care the treacherous lee
  Of rocky shore.

#### II.

Whoever cultivates the golden mean,
  The smirch of poverty shall safely shun,
And mocking riches from his gaze serene,
  Shall ever run.

#### III.

The loftiest pine feels most the northern blast,
  The highest towers endure the greatest fall;
Yon thunderbolt the lesser house has past,
  To strike the tall.

### IV.

Oh! let your soul, prepared for either fate,
   Hope in ill-fortune—fear the prosperous hour;
The self-same gods now kindle, now abate,
   The tempest's power.

### V.

Be sure, if all is dark with you to-day,
   'Twill change to-morrow: songs not always waft
From great Apollo; nor shall always slay
   His vengeful shaft.

### VI.

Oppose a resolute and cheerful breast
   To blasts unprosperous, but be careful too;
Reef sail, when too propitious from the west
   The breezes blow.

## AD FUSCUM.

### I.

The man of pure and upright life,
Needs not the Moorish bow or knife,
Or arrows poison-charged; for he,
O Fuscus, dear to me!
Is safe within his own integrity:

### II.

Whether o'er desert sands he goes,
Or toils through wild Caucasian snows,
Or under burning Persian suns,
The heat of noonday shuns
In groves, through which the bright Hydaspes
    runs.

### III.

For while in Sabine woods I strayed,
And sang my Laura, sweetest maid,
Unarmed, except with fragile lyre,
I met the gray wolf's ire
With fearless gaze, and awed his savage fire.

### IV.

Such omen, never savage clime
Hath known, in this or other time:
Not Daunia's woodlands, nor the land
Of Fez, sirocco-fanned,
Dry nurse of lions; realm of thirsty sand.

### V.

Should I be sent where deadly air,
Malarious, blasts the grape and pear;
Where chilling, endless rain and storm
The drooping skies deform,
And ever shut from sight the sunbeams
    warm;

### VI.

Or where, beneath a torrid sky,
To linger is to faint and die—
Land to all other men denied;
Were Laura by my side,
I with the laughing maid could joyously
    abide.

# HOMER.

*A BALMY gale from far Ionian shore,
That blows throughout the world for evermore.*

BLAND Majesty—that tells the mingled tale
   Of War and Peace, of Marriage and of Death;
Of ruddy Conflagration, Famine pale,
   With sweet, unvaried, and unfaltering breath.

A fragment, unalloyed, of the Divine,
   Who sends the rain to good and bad alike;
Who on the murderer makes his sun to shine,
   Whose fated lightnings oft the righteous strike.

Immortal Singer: thou didst rise above
   Smiles for man's joy, and tears for human pain;
No frailty mars the calm and boundless love
   Which thou for all mankind didst entertain.

## MILTON.

*An organ-peal from far-off Minster walls,*
*That on the awe-struck ear at evening falls.*

BECAUSE you dared to draw aside the veil
   That hides the other world from mortal eye,
And tell, till then untold, the awful tale
   Of man's first sin, that doomed us all to die,

We hail thee Poet: thou art Preacher too;
   With mighty hand you draw the soul away,
Through Death's dark valley, hid with boding yew,
   Far from sweet airs and cheerful light of day.

And yours the Preacher's recompense. We bow
   To thee with reverence; but how few can claim
A friend's acquaintance with thy solemn brow,
   Or in their careless moments speak thy name!

## SHAKSPEARE.

> Symphonious music; orchestral and rare—
> A thousand lutes, and each a separate air.

My Teacher: Teacher thou of all the race—
  And mine as well as theirs: I clasp thy hand,
And look without a fear upon thy face,
  Contented ever in such light to stand.

What men find not upon thy ample page,
  Is worth but little. Would they wiser be?
You speak, and lo, the sum of all things sage.
  Would they be witty, cynic, grave, or free?—

In you is found exhaustless store for all;
  Eternal Record of the Maker's power:
Great Hint of what had been but for the Fall,
  Of what we may be at a Future Hour.

# CYRILLA.

# CYRILLA.

I TELL a simple tale.  The wild romance
Of other age and clime, let him declare,
Whoever sweeps with better, bolder hand
The sacred lyre of song.

      The young Seborne
Had grown to manly age, a farmer's son,
Upon the banks of blue Connecticut.
Fed with the fare the simple country gives
To mind and body ; strong, and lithe, and tall.
His face outshining healthy, innocent thought ;
Yet with a latent gleam that might repel
Whomever would approach with threat or wile.
Fresh-hued and ruddy he with morning air,
And shoulders broad from mowing countless
  meads,
And guiding the slow plough through fallow
  fields.

And patient he till now with rustic toil;
His soul slow waking, yet was satisfied
With labor well fulfilled and rest enjoyed—
With iterative talk of country folk—
With kindly simpleness of village maid,
Rough sport of untaught comrade, and such all
As make the sum of still New England life.

When at the meadow's foot he lay at eve,
And watched the fair blue river flowing by,
He scarcely wished to venture on its breast
And try with it the fortunes of the world.
Than these no meads are sweeter: here are trees,
And hills, and plains, as fair as such can be.
Here, all I know are kind, and labor shared
By all is honor, and joins hand with peace.
Nor here appear the shocks and storms of life;
Nor here does want distress, or pride deform.
And why should I, as others, seek a strange
And unknown world beyond, and turn too late
To seek again the once sure joys of home,
Which, if despised and left, are found no more?

This would he say, unknowing.  Not as yet
Had come to him that stern, relentless voice
That comes at last to all, and drives them forth
To conquer all the earth.  Some fall at first,
Fear-trodden—by the shadow of danger slain;
And those who bravest strive, and longest live,
Attain such portion of their youth's wild dream,
As were a sunbeam's mote to Caucasus!

But though ambition not as yet had crushed
His still contentment, it was not the sleep
Of ignorance in which his wishes lay.
Long had he passed from out the village school,
Whose tall lean belfry, seen the country round,
Fills the young rustic with an uncouth awe,
His sire with pride, when on a winter's night
Its clanging, dissonant bell wakes up the hills,
And to the lecture calls the township in.
Then while the orator—perchance Divine
From some too liberal, half-suspected desk;
Or metaphysic sage, whose thoughts, grown thin,
Lacking the stimulus the public gives
Of praise and pudding, sudden wax robust

When aired upon the platform; poets too,
Who scoring down in grim heroic verse
The follies of the times, their audience spare,
And leave each set of listeners with the thought
Most comforting, that all of mankind else
Wear asses' ears, and quite as loudly bray;—
Then while the orator wears out his hour,
The social cauldron of the busy room
Boils fast, but yet repressed, till at the close
Its pent-up treasures flow o'er all the crowd.
Then gossips mix, then secrets owners change,
Then multitudinous news of nurseries fly;
And in sly corners, hid from dire mammas,
Sweet hours are fixed, when Reuben from the Hill
Shall meet Clarinda, with the skittish bay
Thrice charged with furtive oats, and o'er the lake
Shall ring the steel-shod sledge.

      From village school
He long had passed, but yet the master's skill
Might guide his thoughts, when by the winter's
  hearth
He traced the plots of Euclid, and the path
Of ships upon the unknown ocean drew.

Stoop-shouldered and pedantic was the sage,
And shy, and starting at a sudden voice,
Or sudden step—the more if female too—
And full of musings: of the wrinkled earth,
How many countless ages growing cold,
And fit for use of man; of new-born lands,
Marsupial tenanted, and full of strange
And unfit couplings of the mammal race,
As not yet ripe for view; and of the stars
That once illumed the spaces where the dark
Of void abyss now mocks the straining sight;
And of the era when the constant Bear
Shall wheel a larger circle, and shall dip
Beneath the icy sea, and the clear Lyre
Shall burn throughout the year, the polar star;
And in the summer midnight all the north
Shall see the wonders of the Southern Cross.
Nor had he small pretense of ancient tongue,
But mourning much the village so remote
From Library, where folios kept the key
Of long-passed customs, in default of which
The verse of Persius seems but farrago,
And Plato a sublime, profound, obscure.

So guided, with much wheat his mind was fed,
Somewhat perchance with chaff; but this the clear
And patient thought out-winnowed for itself.
And Nature in him kindly wrought, that he
Might not uncouth become, or turn to dreams,
Or waste away in mists of reverie.
But Knowledge nobly fed his daily thoughts,
Kept all his soul at work, that while the plough
Traced up the furrow, he should trace a truth;
And in the heats of harvest, other sheaves
Than those of barley he should gather in.


The fairest field of all the fair estate
His father owned, lay in the river's bend.
Above, a mile of rapids, and below
A clear, slow flow of water: all the bank
Was alder set, and here and there an oak,
From which all day the shrill kingfisher swooped,
And thrush at dawn and twilight sang; across
Were sloping flats, and parks of meadow land,
In which, knee-deep in richness, countless kine

Strayed at their will; and cottages all white
Peeped from green clumps of trees, and far behind
Low lines of hills arose, enfolding all.

One evening here, when the last furrow turned,
His oxen's heads stretched homeward, the quick stroke
Of rower smote his ear, and down the rifts
Of the swift river shot his cousin's boat,
From Edge, five miles above. "You surely stop,"
He cried, to which, "You're right, no other end
Had I in coming; so my freight commands,
These ladies two, who think it rarest sport
That I should pull an hour's easy oar,
To bring them here, when scarce a summer's day,
And four such men as I, could take them back,
On the same highway."

Then, with dexterous hand,
He shot the skiff within a little cove,
Where the smooth marge an easy landing gave.
And quick, Seborne: "To me will fall the freight,
While you insure the safety of the craft

Within the harbor: such the river's rules,
Which here I claim to follow."

      " This is he,"
Said George of Edge, " whom, ladies, I described
To you a mile above—a bashful youth!
But now I think he knows the water-nymphs,
Who teach him, in these shy, sequestered spots,
Such arts of rhetoric as my three campaigns
On city carpets may have failed to give.
O fairest freight that e'er the river bore!
Be pleased to know your guardian!"
         Bowing low,
He, thus acquainted, led them up the bank,
Whom soon the oarsman followed. Then the yoked
And patient oxen, stretching forth their heads,
Lowed softly toward them, threading through the lane;
Such avenue as who upon thy banks,
Sweet flowing river, has not learned to love?
O'erarched with elms that checked the noonday glare;

A winding maze of blackberry and rose,
And purpling elder; worn with feet of kine,
And giving frequent glimpse of miles of meads.
Soon looms the sturdy barn upon the view,
Four-square; a mass of red—the steep-sloped roof
Mossed o'er with many summers; in the peaks
The diamonds whence the haunting swallows fly;
Beyond, the orchard; last, the glistening house,
A miracle of whiteness: such bequest
Of rustic taste, from heir to heir has come,
Since first the dusky Indian fled the wood,
And left his wigwam as a warning mark,
Which all might shun to copy. Reason else
Is none for this eternal glare of white;
Though yet my memory ever holds it dear,
As first and farthest landmark, when I look
Back o'er the fading slopes of infancy.

Then round the well-spread table, in the dusk,
They told the day's events: how George proposed
The voyage down the rapids; Lucy, then,

Held up her hands in fright, but soon was won
To grasp the project by some dainty lines
From out the "Lady of the Lake," and grown
From timid, venturesome, Cyrilla, too,
Sat on the thwarts unmoved: the only fear
Of both, as now they laughingly confessed,
Their baggage. "Charming care to me," said
    George;
"If dashed by river spray, my pardon I
Had vainly asked. But mostly I obtained
Applause by steering through the foaming rifts
So smoothly, that the songs the Naiads sang
Missed not a quaver, nor were rudely shaken."
And then Seborne: "Such songs, I dare to say,
As ne'er the wistful stream had heard till then;
And now I know the reason that, before
Your boat appeared, or e'er the oars were heard,
Sweet murmurs came upon the northern breeze,
As telling of unwonted melodies:
And vague expectancies filled all my soul."
To which Cyrilla: "Surely, I believe
As George has said: with river-nymphs you talk,

Who teach you flattering arts." "But if you
    knew,"
He said, " the many tongues of solitude,
And how the sense is sharpened by the still
And lonesome airs that o'er the meadows
    breathe,
You would not doubt my story. But if you
Will sing again the songs that down the stream
Crept softly, as if loth in their own sound
To lose what followed from the self-same source,
I then will tell you if I heard them right,
Or if the north wind mocked me."

                        "To the same
Guitar I then will sing," Cyrilla said,
" That you may have, so far, the benefit
Of a resemblance that may haply stir
Your arts inventive; but if I shall say,
' I heard an air that up the rushing stream
Ran boldly, as if glad to run beyond
The dash of water over noisy rocks,'
And then shall ask you to repeat the lay,
' That I may tell you if I heard it right,

Or if the south wind mocked me,' you must
    sing!"
And George replied: "He blushes as if caught;
And thus may ever false deceiver fall!"
But then Cyrilla laughed and said, "And if
He say he heard this song below the rifts,
For witness I shall look to you;" and sang:

  Before the morning woke, the lark
    His warblings scattered through the sky;
  Till night's enfolding deepest dark,
    He sang, nor knew the reason why—
    Such joy disdains a reason why.

  Sweet winds of Spring, that hither blow
    From lands of Palm-tree, warm and dry,
  Beat back the hosts of northern snow,
    And we'll not ask the reason why—
    Such kindness knows no reason why.

"The same, the very same," Seborne replied,
"And yet 'tis not; for there were other lines,
Whose words I caught not, yet their soul and
    sense

Came down to me; a moral to your lay,
As fit for poets."

                    "Not at all," said she;
"The words are not the words above I sang,
Nor do I add a moral to the lay
Which haply in an idle hour I sing."
"And right!" said George, "for this is not the
        mode
By which the poet strikes the hearts of men,
And lives to other times. Let each one frame
A moral as it suits him, but the bard
Sing but of life as actually it lives—
Of nature, simply. If the passions range
Themselves along his verse, he but reviews
Their ranks as Captain—not as meddlesome
And curious gazer, who exclaims, 'Oh! see,'
And 'Wonderful to look upon!' Let each
Admire as it may please him best, and I
Will swear by Homer, who not once complains,
Or sheds a tear, or drops a moral saw,
Though heroes fall by dozens; though the brave
And dear Patroclus lie amid the dust;

Though bright Sarpedon, born of Jove, beneath
A murderous lance expire, and Priam's sons,
Up to great Hector, die the cruel death!
Enough of glory, if the reader mourn.
But if you heard a moral in the winds
To southward sweeping, let it feel the air
Once more, though much I fancy that the breeze
That brought it to you, bore it thence again."

Seborne replied: "Your lecture, learned, wise,
Had given me time to frame a brace of songs,
Had I known none, or breezes been less kind;
And this was not the song Miss Vernon sang,
Nor worthy her—but much the self-same air,
May, if she will, accompany; and sang:

  The friend I left but yesternight,
    To-day seems distant, cold, and strange;
  The little space from light to light
    Hath wrought a sad and endless change—
    For change comes not to such a change.

Dear Heart, in whom my heart I see,
  Shall any Tempter tempt to range?
Content am I to love but thee;
  Nor more could flow from any change—
  Ah! what return from such a change!

"Unkind were you," Cyrilla then replied,
"To say that this was not the song you heard,
By northern breezes blown, else had I used
The arts you practise, and assumed them mine."
"This is the Naiad who inspires him,"
Said George. "No mortal maiden tunes his lay,
And many vouch for this. For to the fair,
Abroad, at home, at church, at every feast,
Full cold is Robert; not the veriest flirt
Has ever claimed him hers a summer hour.
What would I give for such immunity?
Or failing this, the other dear extreme,
The faithful heart, in whom my heart to see
Were blest contentment, and to her the same?"
"Nay, George, you jest," said Lucy; "are you fit
For such contentment—you, who love to play
With female hearts, and idly reckon up

How many here, how many there, have given
The proofs that you were tenderly beheld?
But as for me, I think the proofs are forged;
The scented letters are but party-notes;
And well I know who plucks the rose to-day,
To show its leaves to-morrow with a sigh:
'Ah! were she here, who gave this flower to me!'"

Thus answered Lucy, shaking back her curls,
A sweet defiance darting from her eyes,
As if to say: "You make no sport of me;
Or if you do, no farther shall you stray."
For such the rumor ran, that if the pair
Were not on lovers' footing, plain expressed,
Why, then, as gossips talk, they should be so.
The which Cyrilla told to her that night,
In the great chamber, in the final words
Of that young-lady talk, which, when begun
On such affairs by heads on pillows laid,
Oft in the midnight hour awakes papa,
Who, dimly conscious, robbers fears; perchance
Calls through the house, "Who's there?" So these

In the great chamber talked; the hangings waved,
And trembled to the zephyrs playing through;
The moonbeams slid between the rustling vines
That o'er the windows hung, and paved the floor
With silver arabesque, and the faint stir
Of folded kine crept softly in; and one
Denied, as who has not denied, when urged?
The other with a battery of facts
Resistless charged. The fort is doomed to fall
Where traitor lurks; for Lucy longed to tell
Cyrilla of her heart, the more that she
Were then most safe in George's love, for else
Cyrilla might have smiled; but honor now
Would bind her fast to Lucy's side, and check
Advance of the bold warrior George, who now
Unconscious slumbered, nor had lost his sleep
For such slight cause. The tears that Lucy shed;
Bright nectar of her overflowing heart;
Soon fled away; and then a passing bird—
What else might spy amid such sanctity?—
Had well observed the wondrous wise advice
Of maid to maid, on such momentous theme.
Less must she love, but more must she command

His worship: from her far-off maiden throne,
With unseen forces, draw him up; but she
Must not in aught descend, or let him read
The index of her soul. If he were cold,
She must not sadden: not as meadows show
Black shades of clouds that fly beneath the sun,
Must she be gloomed when hid from sight of him.
If haply he might see his name were prized—
This were the far extent, for love is apt
To cool, if meeting first too much response.
And much more sapience, growing still in weight,
Till from the distant belfry sounded "Two,"
And the spring cocks began to hoarsely crow.
But then as Lucy, burdened with advice,
Slipt into sleep, a last and little word
Rose to the air—"I love him, as he knows."

But when the morning from the distant hills
Stept redly forth, unclouded, all the house
Rose to the matin service, well performed
With reverent reading of the Word, and prayer.
And then the father and the mother sat
At the long table, looking o'er its length,

Each at the other; at the side of each,
The happy children of the bounteous farm,
And the three guests, to whom Seborne proposed
Whatever pleasure that might fit the day—
The journey to the mountains, or the ride
To where the brook in shivering cascades
Falls down the piny side of Cloudycrown;
A sail upon the river, and to add
To this, to land three miles below, and view
The ruins of a fort, whose shady nooks
Once swarmed with musketeers, who kept at bay
A sloop surcharged with red-coats, till the rouse
Of all the country-side compelled to strike
Saint George's flag.

     This pleased the party best;
"And haply," said Cyrilla, "we shall see
The Naiad, if she hear the wonted roll
Of the broad wheels, along the tremulous bank,
Of the ox-wagon. Do not say me no,
Or think it trivial wish that in such wain
I much have wished to travel; not for long,
'Tis true, for much I fear the rugged path

And unaccustomed jolt—yet who has not
Fair picture seen of wagon laden down
With group of vintagers or harvest-girls,
By patient oxen slowly drawn, whose necks
Milk white, obedient bear the yoke, but firm
They plant their hoofs within the faithful ground,
As sure of sturdy succor there."

         Seborne
Replied: " The chestnuts at the door deny
That you should favor the slow foot of ox.
Nor may we lightly lose the morning breeze."
But she: " Thus ever fade romantic dreams,
And us the country soon will hence return
To dusty life amid the city's walls,
Arcadia not yet fully felt; for I
Had dreamed to touch the plough, to ride in cart,
To bind a sheaf, to reap the standing corn,
And scatter seed upon the fresh-turned earth;
But all am I forbid, and rustic ways
Fly from my path—but I shall catch them yet."

But these complaints were lost in air, when now
The chestnuts sprang along the shady lane,

And dashed the morning diamonds from the grass.
From off the meadows newly mown, the lark
Rose, and with poisèd wings across their path,
Clear singing, flew. The summer birds above
Called to each other; and across the stream,
Now silver shining through a belt of trees,
The quarrier's rude refrain from out the hills,
Far distant, floated, softened down to song.

Then on the margin of the stream the boat
Received them, white, and glistening in the sun,
And spotless as its sails, which first Seborne
Shook out, and hauled and fastened without reef—
A shapely flat from gaff to boom; and then,
To all their seats apportioned, he sat down,
And steered the willing boat, that o'er the waves
Flew lightly.

But the maidens docile sat,
As on an element of unknown fear,
Which they are wise who well conciliate,
Nor tempt its unroused powers. Diverse were
   they,

Yet both alike in fairness—oft Seborne
Had Lucy seen, the pride of ancient Edge,
Favored by young and old, and worthy she
The love of all, who all sincerely loved.
The sick her praises sang, who with her bore
A welcome air of health; she seemed to shine
A healing star amid the darkest nights
Of weary folk in mortal anguish.  Light
Her step to such, and bringing hope of rest.
Much cause had he to thank her, for if strange
And shy the village called him, she took up
The welfare of his name, praised what he knew,
And wished that she but knew as much, and they
Might wish the same, were they but wise to wish;
And other such, as women love to talk,
Defending those assailed; though much she blamed
Him to himself in friendly argument,
But with a comic, half-relenting smile,
As all to purpose none; " for who could turn
A stubborn tree, that in the shade persists
To grow, nor yields except to axe and fire?"
And much he loved her; not with vague alarm,
Not with strange leapings of the heart and pulse;

Nor throbs of soul in early morning, when,
From Night and Nothing waked, the eager thought
Quick reaches out for something to recall
Itself to joyous life—then if the maid
Were pictured to the soul at eventide,
She first appears to welcome it to life,
New rising, robed in charms, and breathing warm
Of love, and sighs, and scarcely hoped consent.
Not thus he loved her; clear and well defined
His love, he could have taken it apart,
And pictured forth in strict detail the whole.
And such can rarely grow, and rarely wane,
When once the fair guest-chamber of the soul
Is filled with it. And happy they who find
Such tenant for their heart, for thus they shun
The storms of life, its ecstacy and pain;
There jealousy attacks them not—the fire
That warms them burns with steady equal flame,
Nor soars to heaven to sink in ashes cold;
And haunted not by ghosts of former joys,
They ever breathe the pleasant airs of peace.
While thus she sat, her simple beauty flowed
Over his sense like crystal stream of health,

Making him glad, and only glad, as she
Would wish, if choosing.

     But Cyrilla, strange
And new, as if from other, distant sphere,
Disturbed his soul: for not as other maids
She seemed to him, for something in her face
Appealed to eyes that ne'er before had looked
From out his heart; and voices came from her,
And spoke to ears that never he before
Knew he possessed. As if in former time,
Before this present life, she at his side
Had gone through some great peril, or had spoke
Some passionate words of nearness, dear she
  seemed,
And yet more distant now, than all the maids
Of earth. It were a boldness but to speak
To her: to take her hand in needful courtesy,
Were daring rashness.

     Not the wondrous charm
Was lacking there, of fairness most complete,
As who shall say me nay, who thinks of her,

Who is—or has been—or shall yet be, his?
And such her fairness seemed to him, who yet
Up to that hour had never thought of maid,
Save as a tender, pleasant, kindly friend,
To meet upon the sunlight side of life's
Long street, when weary of the walk in shade,
And dull procession of the toilsome crowd.
And as the boat—while blew the western wind—
Shooting by dexterous tack from bank to bank,
Left long diagonal of babbling wake,
Her eyes, exploring either meadowed shore,
Would oft encounter his, which then the course
Viewed more intently: not as if abashed
And forced to turn away; but sudden sense
Of joy, that might too joyful prove, and turn
To pain, compelled him; but her graceful form
He scanned, less fearful; and if she but drooped
Her eyelids, he was 'ware of it before
They fell, and quick his eager eyes regained
Possession of her face; and so they passed
Three miles of meadow, until Lucy said,
"The Fort!" and rounding to, he dropped the
    sail.

And scarcely had they climbed the ruined steps,
And reached the stone-bestrewed and earthern floor,
Where once the butt of musket rang, and feet
Of sturdy musterers from the market-town
Tramped to and fro in martial exercise,
When other voices reached them ; then Seborne
Said: "'Tis the merchant and his wild Malay,
Who have a pic-nic here, as if a type
Of that bright day when Asia and the West
Shall greet each other. Let us call them out,
And they shall bring the yellow Hoang-Ho,
To mix its waves with blue Connecticut.

For this is he, a summer traveler, who
This season took the Cleveland place, that lies
A mile above—I think, the fairest house
The river sees in all its long descent.
Its owner lives in town, too proud to sell,
Too poor to keep in order as he likes ,
To see it; therefore, as each April comes,
He flits, and draws a rental from the rich,
Whoever comes to taste its summer bloom.
And Beckford is the last, a kindly soul,

Much burned with Indian suns, a bachelor,
And followed by an olive, tall Malay,
Than whom none else can cook his rice or mix
His curry; as for tea, I think that he
Would parch with thirst before that he would
    drink
At his own table, any other cup
Than that which skillful Apposam had mixed!"

But the Malay's quick ear behind the wall
Anticipated their approach, and forth
He came, and called his master.  He, a man
Of portly front, appeared : a picture rich,
Of scarf, and coat, and button; solid all,
As fits substantial men ; but tropic airs
Breathed from him, and he looked the gorgeous
    East.

Then, salutations made, he bade them walk
Within the wall, where piles of rubbish lay,
Profusely scattered; these the nimble hand
Of the swart servant soon disposed in shape,
Each stone and shard in place, and o'er them all
He spread soft shawls, and all the party sat

At lunch; and many stories of the fort
Passed round, perhaps enlarged by lapse of time—
Though scarce the walls were bloodless, and a mound,
Turf-grown, upon the western side, disclosed
And honored the repose of six brave men.

And now and then a tale of the far East
Was told by Beckford; moderation just
He showed, nor ever tired with traveler's talk;
But tropic air, and dress of wild Malay,
Sped all his words, and while he talked, they saw
The minaret; the Indian City; sand
Of tawny desert fringed with spicy shore;
Long swells, and surging waves of yellow sea;
The wild fantastic piles that China builds
Of palace, house; the wondrous Tartar wall.
Then the long voyage to the northern line
Of Eastern commerce, where the summer sun
At midnight on the horizon rolled, and rose
Through orange tints of morning; on the shore
Far off they saw the huts of Samoieds,
And to the north the blink of endless ice.

But while they listened, started up Seborne,
And said : "I fear the march of yonder cloud
Low at the west—it grows apace, and see,
How frequent reft by lightning!" Up they rose,
And filled the homeward boats, and Beckford said,
" Come, let us try a race—perhaps our zeal
Will leave the storm behind." " But let the sheets
Lie in your hand," Seborne replied; " the flaws
Strike sudden on the river, and if fast,
The stubborn sail may bring you on your beam,
Or haply worse." But Beckford said : " Not I,
For I have sailed long wastes of stormy sea,
Beyond the sight of land, in lesser craft,
Nor ever found my hand too slow to loose
The fastened ropes, when down the hissing gale
Swept from the darkened cloud." Then up the
    stream
They flew, the wind athwart; from side to side
The sharp bows cut through ridgy rows of foam,
And still the boat of Beckford led, till now,
When half across a tack, an angry flaw
Struck down from out the east, right in the brow
Of the black cloud that all the western sky

Deformed, and swept long leagues of dust and rain
Before its face.   Scarce in the blinding spray
Was half the ruin seen, for all Seborne
Could spy amid the darkness on the lee
By which he swiftly drove, was a white waste
Of floating sail; and in the windy roar,
He heard the mingled tongues of west and east,
Diverse, but like in tone—the cry for help,
That makes all voices kin.   "Quick to the helm,"
He shouted, "George, and drive, nor try to turn,
But run the boat to shore; a house is near."
Then leaped astern, while George the rudder took,
And shaped the flying madness of the boat,
'Mid spray and rain, till on the clayey shore
It sharply struck, and safe, with dripping haste,
They gained a farm-house.

       But Seborne alone,
Amid the waters seemed, for looking round,
Far as he might, o'er swelling mounds of foam,
He nothing saw, but still swam boldly on,
Where last he saw the sails of Beckford's boat
Flat on the wave; at last, through choking rain,

He dimly caught it; then again more near,
And nearer still, till, clinging to the mast,
He spied the swart Malay, who loudly shrieked,
And pointed out astern. There Beckford fought,
But feebly, with the waves that bore him down,
And once had all engulfed him; but he rose
With final rouse of will, and now again
Was slowly sinking, and had risen no more;
But ere he passed away, the sinewy arm
Stretched by Seborne, had clutched him, and the
    slow
And dragging lift of painful strength had raised
His head to life and air. Nor was there need
Of caution not to struggle; helpless, he,
As infant, and his limbs relaxed and numb;
Then with the current combating, Seborne
Watched for the drifting boat that slowly came,
But came at last, and on its welcome side
He fastened Beckford, faintly brought to life.
But he unshipped a thwart, and used as oar,
And slowly urged the wreck before the storm,
Until, at last, the shore appeared, and safe
They stepped on land; and o'er the flooded fields

And miry ways, they reached the farm-house, where
The others had their welcome gained; and now
The sturdy hinds were setting forth with George,
To try the watery search.

                       But all night long,
In dreams Cyrilla shone upon Seborne,
A water-nymph on peaceful current: when
It dawned, she sank in storm; and faces white
Of drowning men in inky depths of wave,
Flashed ghastly on his sight. A restless fear
Shook all his soul; and, unrefreshed he rose,
And thoughts of peril chased across his mind;
But at the early table, bright and fair
The maids appeared, and talked his praise, but he
Disowned the merit; then the hearty form
Of Beckford, gorgeous as a June parterre,
Saluted him and thanked him; but he bowed
The thanks away, and made a lighter thing
Of all the watery toil, than if with breeze
Of summer he had floated in his boat,
And rescued lady's scarf, blown on the wave.
But when said George, "Good by, to-day we go,"

And Lucy and Cyrilla said, " Good by,"
He knew whence came the sadness that oppressed
His heart before its time : though but an hour
Cyrilla's face had lighted up his path;
Though scarcely had he passed beyond the hedge
Of mere acquaintance, nor had earned the right
To think of her as friend; nor might expect
To live within her memory a day ;
Yet she his life had changed; and though he now
Might never see her more, yet he was not
As once he was, before the maid appeared ;
Nor when they parted, did his soul go back
To where it once reposed.

      The peaceful farm,
And all the bright, green affluence of the meads,
And the fair river flowing to the sea,
Seemed to his eyes to-day a waste expanse
Of earth and water ; but to-morrow they
Might glow as if the heavens had fallen down,
And taken their place. For now Seborne was two
Distinct and separate souls : joyless the one,
With blank, dull eyes, and seeing in no place

The signs of life and hope; its throbs were pain,
Itself a weight upon itself, and lone.
The other saw a radiance everywhere,
That lit up all the world: through cloudy skies
It saw the sun clear shining; in the murk
Of night, the stars beyond: no earthly sound
But seemed a heavenly note; the very air
Played, tremulous with delight, and but to live
Were pleasure, if the same bright sense might last.

But still his outward life moved on, as life
Must move, unless it utterly sink away,
Though nature shock with changes; though the night
Bring death of loved ones in the house; or hearts,
Once faithful, slip away, and empty leave,
And broken, the fair shrines where once they dwelt.
To-day the haying; then the harvest moon
Rose o'er the stubble-field his arm had reaped;
And then in goodly rows the shocks of corn
Told his industrious husbandry; till came
The autumn nights, and sowed the ground with frost.

Then in his labors pausing, more there hung
The cloud upon his soul; and on the bank
Of the blue river, seaward flowing, he
Sat often, musing much; and Beckford came
One day to give a parting greeting; he
Had full outstaid the season; and his chair
In dingy city office waited him.
He who had never dreamed of sentiment,
But lived a life like gorgeous tropic flower,
That drinks in all of light and air it can,
Had watched Seborne with curious eye, and seen
The warpings of his soul, and from the heights
Or depths he occupied, had pitied him;
And finding him, to-day, upon the bank,
Said, as with random shot: "You miss the girls,
Who made the river fairer than itself,
When in your boat they sailed?"

      Then said Seborne:
"I know not what I miss; or if I miss
The faces that I saw but for a day—
I think I only miss the fair content
Smiled by this stream upon me, formerly."

And Beckford said: "My logic teaches this—
There falls no loss without a cause: Content
May fly in thousand ways; but if it fly,
You must pursue; itself it turns not back.
But can a river always please a man?
Or fields, or farms, however fair they be?
And will you waste the unreturning years
Of Youth among the meadows and the hills?
These give not knowledge: if they lend a sense
To see with clearer eye whence beauty springs,
This is their final use; but you should rove,
And mix with busy life. The city street
Will more inform with life and hope, than this
Dull picture of the meads—an office chair
Will teach you more of Man. But better still
Is travel; and no matter where you rove,
The eye instructs the mind; and though you talk
With Turk or Tartar, more the busy sense
Will learn, than if 'twere cooped among the shelves
Of library, or slept amid the vales
Of some such farm as this."

     "A cure, indeed,
For listless or for wounded soul," Seborne

Replied. "Ulysses, in his wanderings, learned
The ways of many men, and ever since
The school has prospered; but am I a king,
Who only needs to speak, to line the shore
With ships, and choose the stateliest? If he go
With drift of fortune, all will follow fast;
And if he sail around the weary globe
For very sport, his escort still will hold.
For travel is a liberal study. I
Lack most the wherewithal to join the school,
And with the stranger, there is only one
That can interpret well: the pocket god,
Who blesses only in his going. He
Is not, as yet, among the deities
Who rule my life."

But Beckford smiled, and said:
"No king am I, and yet I have a ship,
And more than one. The more unfortunate
Am I, amid such times as these, when ships
Lie still by dozens, rotting at the docks,
And in the summer sun the tarry seams
Start open, and the blistered cordage cracks.

But some are busy—one for China sails
Within a month.  To-morrow I must go,
And be her slave : to invoice, manifest,
Devote my soul : and you shall sail in her,
And though you saved my life, I will not force
A favor on you, but as man with man,
Will pay for service.  You can count a gain
Or loss, as well as any, and can sell
A cargo.  This is all the art you need,
'To get the highest, safely.'  I will teach
Details in time.  For you shall merchant turn,
Nor shall it less an honor prove, than if
You led New England with a dreamy pen.
For once I read that wise Pythagoras,
When taunted by the Greeks, 'philosopher'
And 'dreamer,' said in answer, 'He could rise
To be a merchant;' straightway sallied out,
And bought of figs a cargo—I suppose
On credit ; sailed to Egypt : there he sold
The venture at a profit, and returned
Rich and respected.  Riches always make
Philosophy respectable, and I
Believe that naught else does : such sorry stuff

We get from paupers in the State—but now
I own myself beyond my depth, for I
Am only skilled in teas, and dyes, and wine.
But quit the stream, and if the maids remain
Within your fancy—who can drive them out?—
Let fancy bear them forth upon the seas,
And they shall make you hopeful: you shall look
Through darkest storm with courage, if they smile.
And may your chance be happier far than mine;
For she who lit my life when on the sea,
Though I had never spoke of love, and she
Knew never of the peace her image brought
When rising to my soul in stormiest hours,
In one long absence died; a story old
It is, and yet I never loved again—
Till now grown careless, every maid appears
Far different from the maids who shared my youth;
Nor aught afraid, or shy, but free to say
Whate'er they wish, from which, though late, I find
That I am past the hour that charms a maid.
But now good-by, and you shall surely come."

Then in the hasty twilight Beckford went;
And slowly homeward walked Seborne, and mused
Upon the future, and it seemed to him
That all his soul enlarged, as to the East
His fancy called him; then a vision came
Of power and wealth from distant Indies snatched,
And dear rewards at home, the complement
Of all his hopes; but this as quickly fled
Before the trenchant sword of reason; this
Held sway all night, and morning brought again
Fair hopes; and thus his mind divided rule
Oppressed, until at last, he said: " 'Tis best
That I should go, and let what will be, be."

From home 'tis easy for the young to fly,
When Fortune calls them forth. Who does not
    know
The pride of youth, that thinks the voice that calls
Has never called before, as now, to them?
' Did yonder graybeard ever hear the cry,
Yet come to what he is? The form I see,
That brightly leads me on, he coldly views,
Or sees it not at all: and why but that

To me is given a higher privilege—
To know the joys of Fortune?' A decade
Shall pass, and dull his gaze—another race
Succeeds with equal hopes. Immortal she
Who fools them all!

    Seborne the city street
With unaccustomed footstep walked; the crowd
Of eager faces filled him with amaze,
And most, because unending, as a stream
By countless fountains fed; their look was strange,
As if each soul were self-concentrated;
And quick their walk, and skillful trained to turn,
Nor jostle 'mid the sinuous rush. The roar
Undying through the night disturbed his dreams,
And roused to early waking; and the airs
That through the window came, were not the airs
That o'er the meadows swept at morning: these
Were laden down with human histories,
And all their freshness had been snatched away.

Yet one fair thought made all the city peace,
That here Cyrilla dwelt; but not in peace

The thought endured, for pains of sad despair
Made haste to follow; and with troubled heart
He stood within her presence; he surprised
To find her not surprised; for conscious he,
And conscious overmuch, to that extent
That he might think her conscious too, who saw
His face with kindly eyes, but only kind;
But still, that they were kind so soon, was much.

Cyrilla talked of blue Connecticut,
Asked of the household by the flowing stream,
And how was Beckford, and "She wished papa
But knew him; but New York was large, and kept
So many always strangers; much she liked
His large free talk, and gorgeous tropic air,
In him so natural, and wholly free
Of affectation. She had heard from George
But lately, and from Lucy; Lucy, most
Of all the maidens, lovable by maids—
And this her rarest praise—a sweeter flower
Had never grown upon New England soil."
Through this they grew acquaint, and wandered off
To other talk, and thus the half-hour passed.

But leaving where she dwelt, through doubt and
    fear, .
He could not call himself unwelcome; this
Took half the darkness from his soul—the rest
Remained, to yield a hiding-place to all
The uncouth shapes that vex a young man's heart,
When in the springing time of love he lives,
Not knowing how he loves, or by whom loved.
Then found he Beckford, hid in rosy heaps
Of glowing scarfs, while at the vessel's side
He chode the captain for his long delay.
"And I am idler too," broke in Seborne;
And Beckford greeted him, and said: "The ship
Must lie a fortnight yet, the captain says,
And after that, how long! for never yet
Did captain keep a promised sailing day."
Thus Beckford growled; but then the sailor said:
"The wind that's best is not yet hatched, and I
Will beat the ship that sails to-day, or else
Will forfeit all my share." Then said Seborne:
"The time is given to me that you should teach
The mysteries of the manifest, that I
May rightly learn the rare device of trade."

So all that day he bent with studious eye
O'er formulas of trade, until his brain
Grew cloudy with excess of learning; then
To dine with Beckford, and an evening's stroll
Down the gay avenue, where the rushing crowd,
And roaring whirl of wheels, and miles of lamps,
Aroused him with delight. "To-night the lark
Of Italy sings," said Beckford; "let us go."
They entered as the curtain rose; the band
Of Druids thronged upon the stage, and sang
Of vengeance to the Roman, and they passed;
But with the Priestess soon returned, and she
Sang Casta Diva. Like a bright parterre
In the dead calm of summer noon, before
The thunder breaks, the circled audience held
Itself in silence, till at last applause
In whirlwinds burst. With the sweet song entranced,
Seborne bent down his head, and mused awhile,
  until
The noisy babble of the gay *entr'acte*
Aroused him to the world, and looking up
He saw Cyrilla; with her, Lucy. Then
Came George, fresh smiling, with them both shook
  hands,

And said: "You'll join us in the box?" Seborne
Chanced to Cyrilla's side. Between the scenes
They talked; and when the martial trumpets blew,
And when the two fair women, like in love,
Alike in noble anger, and alike
In the sweet yearn toward innocent infancy,
Fell to each other with sad, passionate song,
Her kindling eye and glowing cheek aroused
His dawning soul; another step his heart
Advanced toward courage; For she feels as I,
He whispered to himself, and fearfully
He nursed the thought, and breathed the balmy
    airs
That floated from her, with a blameless mind.

But parting in the lobby, Lucy said:
"We came but hastily, but we stay awhile;
Come you and see us, and Cyrilla, too,
Our hostess, seconds our request. Full soon
You go to sea, and then who knows how long
Before we see you? But before you go,
Charm not the ears of George with idle talk;
Too well he loves to wander. Should he go,

The dreadful uncle of the story-book
Would clip his portion." Then a finger shook
At George, who laughed, and drew a closer arm.

But one day Beckford said: "The vessel sails
To-morrow, if I live; the long delay
Hath but one compensation, that it keeps
You here, whom I shall miss; but now the times
Brook not a longer stay; the wind blows south
With steady purpose; what the cargo lacks
Of fullness, let it lack; to-night, good by
To your fair friends be said: if younger I,
And forced to leave such pleasant smiles, to sail
To the underworld, why then, since must is must,
I should create of it a comedy,
And with a smiling air take leave, as if
I were but going to the market-town.
And faith, the world is small, and every port
Is home, while you are there: needs not that you
Must ever go where other folk are not;
Meat, drink, and shelter meet one everywhere;
And I have never heard of any place
Where there was likelihood of tumbling off."

Perhaps a volume of philosophy
He might have uttered; but upon the face
Of him who scarcely listened, he perceived
A blank regard, at which he said, " Well, well,
Come down to-morrow early," then wheeled round,
And plunged into a letter.

     But Seborne
Went sadly in the evening to the house
Where late a brighter light had shone than all
The world beside could furnish. If the month
Had quickly flown, yet every night had been
Itself, and many of the evenings he
Had thickly planted with the memories
Of fair Cyrilla. She had fallen to him
Oftener than he had dared to hope, for George
Thought more than he should dare to think, and
   gave
Himself to Lucy most; and she, in play
And earnest both, exacted countless dues.
Now they must part; but more than parting pained
His heart this thought, that parting should be pain.
It seemed a wrong to her, who knew it not,

That even in his most unuttered soul,
He should in such a way associate
Herself with him, as make it pain to part.
Then all the weary changes of true love
In heart ingenuous, rang within his breast—
Unworthy he of this bright soul's regard;
Yet worthy, if she counted love of worth.
But did he truly love? And if he loved
Most truly, had he right to love? Or if
To love were right, were there from thence the right
To give expression, even to that degree
Whence its expression might be faintly seen,
If Love's clear watchman looked from out her eyes,
But else quite unperceived? Such endless chimes
Pealed from the belfry where his passion rocked,
And thrilled his fearful heart.

      If happiness
Be found in love requited, yet the road
Is often thornier than the dim by-paths
That lead through crooked Folly. He who walks
In cynic armor clad, may laugh at thorns,

And brush aside the pains that strike the heart
Of him who, guileless, only looks to love
For his defense.

    The happy hours Seborne
Had known of late, had each an underweight
Of sadness carried; and now, flying off,
They left the burden, harder to be borne,
From the dark contrast.

      Solace there was none
In love, that gave instead a deeper pang.
Had not he loved, he had been happy now,
Or not, at least, unhappy. Fair content
He could have been contented with; but now
Her form had fled, and love, of hope bereft,
Remained, and only to affright and wound.

But all this passed, when now once more he stood
Within her presence, and her frank, sweet voice
Composed his soul. She at her music sat,
And sang a song of winter: how the lake
Lay, a long sheet of ice; the snowy hills
Leaned back on either side, and echoed down

The ring of skaters; till the northern stars
In bright auroras faded.  Then she ceased,
And said: "But you are going to the land
Where winter never comes, and you will miss
The frosty skies, and miss the ringing ice
Of cold Connecticut."

"Too soon I go,"
Seborne replied. "To-night I bid good-by;
The vessel sails to-morrow." Then her cheek
Paled, as if something struck her at the heart,
But quick regained its color; and she said:
"But you must wait for George and Lucy; they
Will not forgive me if you go, good-by
Not said to them; and they will soon be here."


And then she sang a song of Eastern life,
As far toward China as romance has flowed,
A lay of Cashmere; sweet the words, though
  wrought
Into a language not their own; and sweet
The melody, which once a scholar heard,
And brought it home; a simple pastoral tune,

Breathing of mountain air.  A rustic maid
Mourned for her lover, to the Ganges gone,
And lost in myriad masses round the king ;
But either he will die, she said, or else
Return a prince ; for he will ne'er content
Himself to be a soldier in the throng.

This turned the talk awhile.  Cyrilla most
The conversation held ; nor was Seborne
Unapt to silence, for he looked at all
That he must leave, and sorrow filled his heart ;
Nor ever had she looked so beautiful,
Nor ever seemed so near—and far away.

And while he vaguely talked, he wondered if
She felt in least degree the love that now
Consumed his soul, and yet so cheerful she.
And yet he answered, Not a word of love
Have I declared, or lived in any act,
Though full of love.  But if she love the least,
How might she question if I loved at all ;
Who not disclose the passion of my heart,
As most becomes a man : but this I fear

More than all other ending, to disturb
The sphere wherein she sits. If I invade
Its crystal sanctity, what jarring wreck
Might I not make? And this must make me dumb,
Till strength no longer can restrain. But this
Can never be, for soon I go, and leave
The hour and place of possible dismay
Forever far behind. Then with a start,
That brought a wondering blush to the fair cheek
Of her who looked, he woke from out his dream,
And gayly talked, till George and Lucy came,
And brought the hour of parting: then farewell
Came: dreary, commonplace, and profitless end
To friendship bright, that merited other close.

But in the night, the thought of what " farewell "
Might in its long uncertainty contain,
Oppressed him wakeful; and in dreams it stalked
The front of every vision. With the sun
He rose, and sought the ship. The laggard crew
Unwilling thronged; but as the morning warmed,
Came Beckford, with the many short last words
Of business and of friendship. Then the ship

Heaved up her mighty anchor from the stream,
And sailed to sea.  The winter sun went down,
Behind the heights of cloudy Neversink,
And when it rose, no more the Western world
He saw.

    Cyrilla, as the days went by,
The more when George and Lucy took away
Themselves, and that warm air of confidence
In which they lived, a strange and unknown want
Perceived, which not diminished with the days,
But rather grew.  Oft at the window she
Would stand, while spring's slow twilight faded out,
As if expectant of a step, a form,
That never came.  Nor did she dare to ask
Herself what form or step.  Her eyes lacked not
Their usual brightness; rosy was her cheek
As when she sailed on blue Connecticut;
And in her lived and spoke the rich warm blood
Strongly and beautifully : but her heart
Had something gained and lost.  No more in rest
Of bountiful self-content it lived.  From out
Herself, in mode unwonted, she had gone,

Nor knew how much, though hoped it was but
    slight,
As easier to return; but as she tried,
She found the effort vain; nor could regain
Herself, as once she was. Nor was it pain
To wander, but the verge of joy, that yet
Might hint of anguish, if she roved too far.

O'er the round world the vessel sped, and sank
The northern skies behind: then first Seborne
The diamond-dusted Austral pole beheld,
And fair Canopus and the blazing Cross,
Which more than tropic breezes, or the swell
Of boundless seas, recalled his long exile,
And actual breadth of journey. But through all
Despondency of distance, lonesomeness,
Heart-sinkings, fear, and dread of stranger land,
There cheered him one bright thought, that he
    should win
A manly name and fortune, then with these
The brightest might be grasped; nor dreamed how
    much
Of pride lay hid within his love.

                    Through calm
And storm of the Atlantic, summer swell
Of Indian sea, and treacherous western wind
From Asia, fretting o'er the Chinese main,
He came to far Canton, his journey's end.
There, letters found from Beckford, proving all
The grasp of merchant's mind.  Each slight detail
Was noted there, and caution, terse and sharp,
Against a thousand dangers.  "If you weigh
These hints aright," said Beckford, "you will save
Five years of life—for merchant life is judged
By its results in wealth and power; and I,
From fifteen years abroad, drop five as lost.
Had I possessed adviser, who had said,
Thus far, no farther, when the judgment reeled,
By young ambition tempted, I had saved
Those years, and much of suffering, when the soul,
Stung through with sense of injury from trust
Abused, from generous impulse turned to feed
Dishonest cravings, back upon itself
In dark misanthropy recoils.  What charms
Another's money has, not yet you know;
But they about you know, upon whose brows

The lines of Care or Covetousness are writ:
Beware of haggard faces, and of eyes
In which cold Speculation sits; of tongues
Too sudden friendly: he is best your friend
Whom time draws slowly: and beware of plans
Too prosperous-promising. Nature's laws are fixed
Of seed-time, labor, harvest: he who thinks
To break her laws, may break the laws of trade,
And if you take his pledges for the one,
Why—take them for the other." Then went back
To crisp details of trade, and made a close.

But other letters came, from time to time;
Warm throbs from parents' hearts, and kindly
    words
From George and Lucy. When the year was old,
They wrote as one: from time to time a line
Dropped, of Cyrilla; often as his eye
Roved down the newly-opened sheet, and caught
Her name, he felt a numbing shock of fear
Of news which still delayed. Cyrilla fair,
Cyrilla rich, and by the Graces loved—
It fevered him that year was linked to year,

And still a hope for him. His fancy leaped
The barriers of the huge round world; he saw
Each day the maid. To-day, she seemed to smile,
Alone and musing; but to-morrow, she
Was sad amid the gay; another day,
And she led all in mirthfulness, in all
A maiden heart, and void of all regards,
But such as fit the maid who smiles on all
Alike, and passion-free.

     The fifth long year
Had nearly passed, and guided by the clear
And watchful mind of Beckford, who with care
And diligence close surveyed his path, and taught
Just when to profit by the seeming risk,
And when to shut his eyes to seeming gain,
He found one day that he could say, " Enough,
At least for now." The limit he had placed
Was overpast—now, not to lose, was all
He might desire—and though the natural goal
Of five years' journey, roused a glad surprise
Within his heart. He gave a month to ease,
Borne by swift sails to where the last Japan

Shrinks from the frozen sea.  When now again
The shores of China drew together at
The river's yellow mouth, and in the night
The low broad light of far Canton appeared,
He mused, " 'Tis for the last, if this be true."
And by the cabin-lamp the last time proved
The undeceiving balance, where his wealth
Was curtly written.

    In a lesser bark
Than that which bore him out, he sailed for home;
Small, sharp, a clipper, and for swiftness famed;
As he had written: " Scarcely will the news,
By steamer, reach you of my voyage hence,
Before the Glance shall anchor in the bay."
And now he passed Good Hopé, and now the
  Trades,
And now Azores; and now thy stormy crests,
Atlantic, cold and dreary, lay between
The homeward ship and shore.  With careful
  watch,
The master steered the bark, already passed
Within Newfoundland mists.  The luminous

Gray icebergs, southward floating, neighbored them,
As in the fogs they swung.  Three days and nights,
In which the sky seemed melting in the wave,
They drifted idly; at the last, a breeze
Sprang up, and bare them on.

                    But in the night
They felt a sudden shock, and instantly
A riving crash, that thrilled through all the bark;
And in the dark up-rushing, they discerned
A mighty bulk amidships: then a cry
Came from above, mingled and dissonant voice
Of sailors: "Are you sinking?—here are ropes—
Save while we may!—how came your vessel there—
And who are you that cross a steamer's track,
Thus tempting Death, as if the deadly sea
Had not enough of peril?"  Then cried out
The master: "Do not leave us, for the sea
Pours in apace—all shall be roused at once—
Have all in readiness, hang out all your lights!"
Then sped below, to search that none remained,

While at the ropes the willing sailors drew,
And all were saved. But when they all were safe,
The Glance fell off, and slowly sinking, drove
Night-deep in fog, and straight was lost to view.

But when the chill late morning lit the mist
With wan and yellow glare, there came up one
From out the hold, who cried: "A leak—a leak
Hard by the bows! I heard the water plunge
Like cataract!" At the word they all grew pale,
Quick crowding to the hold to know the worst;
But stopped as struck, when trembling, with white
    face,
A fireman struggled up, and gasped: "A leak,
That soon will drown the fires!" Then arose
The cry of shipwreck, than the battle-cry
More fearful—worse than cry of sack and siege,
When through the breach the drunken victors
    urge,
And women die of fear!

    With lips compressed,
The master strove to keep the swarming crew

From off the boats; but mutiny apace
Put on the cloak of irrepressible fear;
Two boats they cut away, and down the side
Clambering pell-mell, thronged in, and one bore off
Into the misty morning. One was swamped
In sight, and no compassion drew, but fierce
And savage curses from the crowd that swayed
Upon the steamer's deck. Some headlong leaped
To gain it, but the icy water chilled;
And sullen ripples marked the place of death.
Three boats remained; at each, with vigilant guard,
Stood two brave men with arms, from whom the
    crowd
Recoiled, dismayed. To these the women came,
Escorted by strong shoulders, 'mid the crowd,
That selfish urged. When now the last was full,
The others lowered, a quick and passionate rush
Surged toward it; but Seborne beat back the crowd
With pistol-butt, and threat of death, until,
When they perceived the boat had struck the wave,
A madness seized them, and a cutlass gleamed,
And clove his cap, and stunned him, and they seized
And threw him, and he fell before the boat

That swiftly rowed for life. Scarce did it stop
To take him in; but one exclaimed: " 'Tis he,
Who saved us all, and it were deepest shame
That he should perish!" Then they drew him in,
And laid his head upon a woman's lap,
To bring him back to life; and as he oped
His eyes, he knew Cyrilla!

      Other chance
Of meeting had amazed them, but the wreck
Made all chance possible; amid the dread
Unknown of waters, blank dismayed surprise
Could be surprised no more. A moment's gaze
To prove her eyes, and then she said: "And you—
Who kept the sailors from the boat! The wound—
Oh! is it deadly? Tell me, did you see
In either boat, my father? In the wild
And final struggle for our lives, I swooned,
And nothing knew until I found me here,
Already loosened from the ship. Not he
It was who struggling in the waves, an oar
Clutched, ghostly pale, and frantically tried
To draw himself within; oh! no, for him

Another seized, just drowning, and they both
Forever sank with such a cry, that I
Had gladly died, had I not heard it. Sure,
My father must be somewhere safe. The ship
Will float—oh! will it not?—or, there are spars—
How many have been saved on spars from wrecks,
As I have read, or floated long on keels
Of vessels overturned, and drifted down
To warmer seas, till found." And while she spoke,
On the still water came to them a wave
Of mighty curve, and followed by a host
Of lesser waves; and these went on, and all
Was still; and then the pallid steersman said:
" May God have mercy—the good ship has sunk!"

Then said Cyrilla: " Is it so?" Seborne
Replied: "An iceberg may have toppled, else
The word is true; but I have hope in this,
That if your father be not in a boat,
He may have caught a fragment of the wreck—
And many vessels sail upon this track."
But then Cyrilla turned away, and hid
Her face within her veil, and silent mourned;
And all that day, and all the night, she mourned.

But when the dreary dark had passed, the mist
Rose up, and showed the sea.  The kindly sun
Beamed warm upon them, and their stiffened limbs
Relaxed.  The chiefest man among them said:
"Friends, let us hope, for we have bread for days,
And water; and the sea and sky seem kind ;
And if they be, to run through six full days,
Will land us : therefore let us all take heart."

Then each a measure of bread and water took,
Just sixteen souls in all; and those at oars
Changed hourly.  Respite scant to those who urge
Their strength against Atlantic!  Ere the noon,
All hearts were knit together, eye to eye
Beamed friendly, and the cheerful word went round
Of how much sea was passed, and wise was he
Who well had stored the boat; and how the bergs
Were fully passed; and would the fogs arise
Again before they landed ?  It was good
The compass had not broken, in the crowd ;
And, here are sea-weeds, let each take a leaf—
Hereafter they shall mind us of our cruise.

And when Seborne had told Cyrilla all

His years abroad, and how his life had sped,
He said: "And you upon the sea!" And she:
"A month's short flight we took, but meant again
To visit more at large the Eastern world.
My father just had laid his cares aside
In rounding up this trip. He often said
That this would end his cares, and death's sad voice
Confirmed it. Has the air grown warm? I feel
Oppressed, and yet my neighbor says 'tis cold."

And then Seborne perceived that fever burned
Upon her cheek, and said to her: "The day
Is weary feverish, after mortal pain,
Unless one sleep." But she replied: "I keep
Such peace for night—oh! to anticipate
The blessing now, and pass the dreadful dark
Awake, amid the blackness of the sky,
And hearing nothing but the rush of waves,
And painful oars, slow moving—then I fear
The memory of the drowning cry would add
To all, till past endurance."

But Seborne
Saw how the fever mounted; as the night
Drew down, he said to one who near her sat:

" Be watchful of Miss Vernon, for there grows
A fever on her—shield her from the damps :
And here is water that I saved for her."
And she replied : " And I have seen the same,
And I will hold her in my arms to-night."

And when the second morning came, she lay
In fever, knowing nothing of her life,
Nor where she was.  Seborne grew sick at heart,
And all felt fear; for here in other shape
Had Death attacked them ; remedy was none,
Beyond the sorely wounded powers of life.
And all day long they pulled a weary oar
From out the blank horizon, toward the blank
Of endless space beyond, that showed no hope.

But when the third day came, the darkened sky
Made threat of storm ; and soon the troubled swell
Broke into waves before the eastern gale.
Heavily the boat was laden, and the seams
Gaped, while she fell from wave to wave ; and one
Incessant baled, and kept the water down,
That else had swamped them.  Chill and blinding
  rain

Beat fiercely on them, and they feared the night.
But God was merciful, and though the night
Lacked nothing of the dangers of the day,
And blackness added, yet the morning found
The boat still driving shoreward through the storm.

But one among the women, to Seborne
Crept in the dusk of dawn, and said to him:
"The fever rages wildly; if I know
Of fever aught, who mourn two sisters fair,
In one short week by this dread enemy slain,
The maid must die, unless the fever change
To-day. And are you not of nearer kin,
Than thus to leave the charge so much to us?
For much she talks of certain places, times,
Where you appear. Oh! take her hand in yours,
And soothe her—with her fancies chime: perhaps
You may with happy circumstance of words
Charm her to quiet." And Seborne came near,
And sat him down amid the hurtling storm,
Beside her, took her hand in his, and gazed
Beneath the roof of cloaks upon her face,
Which thus was scantly sheltered. Fever there
Had traced its deathly mark; and though his soul

Shook with unknown dismay, he calmed his voice,
And favored every fancy she recalled
Of former time in her delirium.  She
Came to his name, and bending low, as if
To guard her maiden soul with manly shield,
He heard the history of her heart; amazed
To find himself therein, and written there
In cipher of which Love alone the key
Possessed.  And most he wondered that she knew
Himself as others knew him not.  For he
To them lived only by his acts: she knew
His thoughts, his close-concealed resolves, and all
That made his guarded inner self, by which
He lived his separate, individual life,
As differing from another.  All the day
And all the night her fevered fancy roved;
But with the fifth sad morning she awoke,
And knew herself, and knew full well that she
Was called by Death.

Then to Seborne she said:
" A long and weary dream I just have dreamed,
But brighter at the close.  You have been near
While I have slept; and tell me now, dear friend,

In all sincereness, have I aught complained,
Or said a word to wound these kindly folk,
Who, 'mid the storm and peril of the sea,
Have given me more than is my rightful share
Of shelter and of room?"

     And he replied:
" Not so, but rather thanks: but most your life
In former times you traversed; and since I
Through one bright month walked by your path
  of life,
I met such mention, which for me to hear
Was most profound of melancholy joy,
Which I am sure that no one else has heard.
And now forgive, that I have said thus much;
Had I said less, I had not truly spoke,
As you required, in all sincerity."

"Dear friend," she said, "I thank you that in this,
You speak as honoring me; a lesser soul
Had covered this. I feel that I must die,
But life is long for you. Grieve not too much
That we have lost what might have been. Per-
  haps,

Though faintly dare I hope, my father lives,
And you will meet: such friendship will be yours,
As flows from sad events together borne,
The life-long moments of the reeling wreck,
And sinking crowds—and death! Such sights, as, shared,
Make kin of all. Your hand—I faint," she said,
And sinking, as he caught her, seemed to sleep;
But in his heart he knew that it was death.


And when the evening sun was low, they saw,
Through mist and rain, the gloomy land ahead,
Waste, scarred by storm. Nor longer had the boat
Withstood the shock of sea. Within a cove
They beached, and drew the keel high up on shore,
And slept a weary sleep, till morning came,
While one sad watcher by Cyrilla sat.


Then, ere they set their faces to the south,
Through leagues of wilderness, they laid her form

To rest beneath the gray and lichened rocks,
Where with unceasing sound Atlantic pours
Its mighty tides.

Such funeral she had.

www.ingramcontent.com/pod-product-compliance
Lightning Source LLC
Chambersburg PA
CBHW032103230426
43672CB00009B/1627